Diary of a Social Detective

Real-life tales of mystery, intrigue and interpersonal adventure

Jeffrey E. Jessum, Ph.D.

PUBLISHING

© 2011 AAPC
P.O. Box 23173
Shawnee Mission, Kansas 66283-0173
www.aapcpublishing.net

Publisher's Cataloging-in-Publication

Jessum, Jeffrey E.
    Diary of a social detective : real-life tales of mystery, intrigue and interpersonal adventure / Jeffrey E. Jessum. -- Shawnee Mission, Kan. : Autism Asperger Pub. Co., c2011.

        p. ; cm.
        ISBN: 978-1-934575-71-0
        LCCN: 2010941755
        Summary: Social skills lessons for young people presented in a narrative text with each chapter focusing on a special topic. Readers are encouraged to help solve social mysteries, fill out worksheets, etc.

        1. Autistic children--Life skills guides--Juvenile literature.
    2. Autistic children--Behavior modification--Juvenile literature.
    3. Autism spectrum disorders--Patients--Behavior modification--Juvenile literature. 4. Children with social disabilities--Behavior modification--Juvenile literature. 5. Interpersonal relations in children--Juvenile literature. 6. Social interaction in children--Juvenile literature. 7. [Autism--Life skills guides. 8. Interpersonal relations. 9. Social isolation.] I. Title.

RJ506.A9 J47 2011
618.92/85882--dc22   1012

This book is designed in Palatino and Futura.

Cover and interior art © istockphoto.com

Printed in the United States of America.

Dedication

This book is dedicated to my angels, Anya and Kaia. May all the mysteries in your lives lead you on wonderful, rewarding adventures, and may you always have the resources and support you need to succeed.

Acknowledgments

Special thanks to Roshan for all her support and encouragement in writing this book. Thanks to my friend and mentor Robert Colegrove, who has enriched my life both personally and professionally over the years. And thank you to all the kids I've had the honor of helping become their own social detectives.

Table of Contents

Introduction

The Making of a Detective

Johnny didn't plan on becoming a detective. What he imagined pretty much every day was being a regular kid, just like everyone else. In fact, for a long time the only thing Johnny really wanted was to be like everyone else. But life had different plans for him.

Ever since he was little, Johnny had trouble fitting in. It seemed that wherever he went and whoever he was with, things went wrong. On good days, the other kids would just ignore him, but more often than not, his social world consisted of a healthy dose of teasing, insults, rejection and bullying. He even had a nickname, "Johnny Strange," which, no matter how hard he tried, he could not shake.

Johnny was a smart kid and knew a lot about a lot of things. But when it came to friends and fitting in, he was lost. The social world was a complete mystery to him. So Johnny ended up spending most of his time alone, where it was safe. He would read and play his favorite video games. In fact, in the world of video games Johnny was a superhero. He loved playing games where he could become a character and solve puzzles and uncover clues. And he loved reading detective books. Most of the time, when he was reading a good detective book, Johnny could solve the mystery way before the detective in the book.

"Why is it so easy for me to solve the mysteries and puzzles in my books and computer games and so hard for me to solve the mystery of kids?" he asked himself over and over.

The harder things got with the kids at school and in the neighborhood, the deeper Johnny went into his computer games and books. But the books and computer games did not fill him up. What he really wanted was to fit in, to not be Johnny Strange. He would try to tell himself he didn't care, but he was too smart to really believe that. He was too smart to forget that all he really ever wanted was to be a regular kid, just like everyone else.

The truth was that Johnny was lonely and, while he had solved countless mysteries and puzzles in his day, the one mystery that was most important, the social mystery, still stumped him.

As he got older, the social puzzles became increasingly challenging for Johnny. He became more and more hopeless about ever fitting in. Life seemed bleak until one day Johnny realized something that would change his life.

"Maybe I've been going about things all wrong," he thought to himself. "Every time I have problems with other kids, I put more energy into my games and books, and every time I put more energy into my games and books, I get better at solving puzzles and mysteries. Maybe what I need to do is think about this social mystery the same way I think about the mysteries in my books and games."

As this thought went through Johnny's mind, a light went on inside of him. It was a light that, once on, never went off again. It was a light that would help guide his way out of the loneliness he had been feeling for so long. It was then and there that Johnny vowed to himself he would not stop until he solved the most important mystery that had come his way yet.

"All the other mysteries and puzzles have been training me for this," he told himself. "Just as Sherlock Holmes solved the mysteries of the crime world, I, Johnny Multony, will solve the mysteries of the social world."

All good detectives have a set of procedures they use to solve their mysteries, so the first thing Johnny did after having this realization was to devise a game plan. He started a list, "Procedures for Solving Social Mysteries." Good detectives start with the facts, and that is where Johnny knew he should start.

So the first part of his procedures list was about gathering the facts.

Six Steps for Gathering Facts

Johnny came up with six important points for gathering facts.

1. **Collect all the facts and write them down.** All good detectives collect the facts and write them down so they can go over them later. (Johnny got a special notebook that he dedicated to solving social mysteries.)

2. **Always have your eyes and ears open for clues.** A good detective realizes that you never know where a really important clue might be hiding.

3. **Pay good attention and always listen carefully, not just to what people are saying, but also to how they say it.** A good detective knows that it is not just words that give you information; it is actions as well. So you want to make sure to pay attention to things like body language and facial expressions, as well as to words.

4. **Always try to look at things from other people's points of view.** Kids always seemed to see things differently than Johnny did. If he could start to understand the way that other kids saw him and saw social situations around them, it might give him important clues for how to solve social puzzles.

5. **Look for clues in the surrounding events.** Often clues can be found in the events that come before and the events that follow a social mystery. For that reason, a good social detective must always think about the events that surround the puzzle he is trying to solve.

6. **Always check the facts.** A good detective always checks to make sure he has his facts straight. He could do this by asking other people how they saw situations, to see if what they saw matched what he saw.

Five Steps for Making Sense of the Facts

The second part of Johnny's list of procedures was about what you do with the facts once you have gathered them. He came up with five important procedures for making sense of the facts.

1. **Break things down into pieces to make them more manageable and easier to understand.** Johnny would frequently get overwhelmed with his social puzzles. They seemed so big and unmanageable, so breaking things down seemed like a good plan.

2. **Imagine how others might be seeing the situation.** Not only does this give you very important facts, it also helps tremendously in understanding and solving social mysteries. This is often called "putting yourself in other people's

shoes," and it can be done in different ways. One way is to ask others directly how they see things. Another way is to imagine that you are that other person and try to see things the way they do. Then ask yourself how you might feel or what you might think if you were them.

3. **Make sure to look at *all* the evidence.** Sometimes it is easy to leave out information that is essential for solving a mystery. For example, if we leave out how someone else sees a situation and only see it from our point of view, we don't have all the clues to understanding what is going on.

4. **Go over the evidence many times and try to see things from as many different points of view as possible.** Good detectives know that we don't always notice all the clues the first time we look over the facts. By examining the facts several times, we can avoid missing things that might be important for solving our social mysteries. Imagining how the facts would look from different points of view can also help us find clues we may have missed the first time around.

5. **Ask for others' opinions.** Two heads are often much better than one, so after examining the evidence, it can be extremely helpful to discuss what you have found with other people in order to get a fresh perspective that might help you solve the mystery.

Introduction
Creating Social Remedies

Johnny realized that being a good social detective was not just about understanding why things happened. To be a good detective, it was also important to find ways of fixing the problems that were going on in his social world. Clearly, the first steps in fixing a problem would be to identify what it was and then to understand why it was happening. Gathering the facts and making sense of them would help him do this.

But Johnny needed to know what to do next. He needed solutions to make his social world better. So he created the last part of his set of procedures, which he called "Creating Social Remedies." A remedy is something that corrects a problem, and it seemed logical to Johnny that, when coming up with a remedy, some important things needed to be done to make sure it worked.

1. It's always helpful to have choices so, after the problem had been identified and understood, Johnny thought he should come up with at least three possible remedies for dealing with it. To do this, he would first brainstorm as many remedies as he could. He would be as creative and imaginative as possible. Then he would narrow down his choices to the top three that seemed to make the most sense.

2. The next step would be to think of all the pros and cons of each remedy. Johnny did this by acting out the situation in his mind and thinking of all the possibilities that might occur if he used his remedy.

3. Johnny thought that another good way of exploring the pros and cons would be to share his remedy with someone he trusted, and ask them what pros and cons they might see.

4. His next step would be to create an experiment to test out his remedy. This would be some social situation in which he could see if his new strategy helped in solving his social problem.

5. Once his remedy had been tested, Johnny would analyze how it worked, taking lots of notes about how his remedy was successful and how it was not. He would notice if his remedy had any positive or negative side effects. If his remedy was not perfect, Johnny would try to learn from it and use the facts that came from it to create a new remedy.

Doing the Detective Work

Johnny was excited about his approach to things. His set of procedures made him feel less overwhelmed about his situation. Now he had a plan, and he always seemed to do better when he had a plan and knew exactly what he was supposed to be doing.

He knew that it might take time, but he was determined to solve this social mystery. He wrote all his procedures on the very first page of his new detective notebook and stuffed the book into his pocket. He went to school with the mind of a detective, believing that he was going to solve this problem just as he solved all his video games and book mysteries. He began to see school and all the mysteries and puzzles it presented as an exciting challenge rather than as an overwhelming, unsolvable mystery.

And while he kept his attention on his academics (academics were never a problem for Johnny), he put extra effort into being aware of what was going on around him. He carried his notebook with him everywhere, taking notes continuously throughout the day and using his six steps for gathering information. At night after completing his school work, he would spend hours analyzing the information he had gathered, using the tools he had created for making sense of the facts.

Slowly but surely, things became clearer to Johnny. He started understanding things in a deeper way than he ever had before, and little by little he began seeing things not only from his own point of view but also from the points of view of other people.

He started understanding how other people were seeing him and his actions, and how other people might be feeling about things. Being able to see things from other people's points of view changed Johnny in an amazing way. He began to realize that he had a tremendous amount of power over his social world. The power came from understanding how things worked, and realizing how much impact his actions really had on how people saw him.

Little by little, Johnny began devising remedies and testing them out. Sometimes his remedies didn't work, but he would always try again. He had never given up at a video game or a detective story, and he sure was not going to give up now. Gradually, he developed a whole medicine chest of social remedies that seemed to be effective in dealing with the social problems he had been having in school year after year.

Johnny was finally getting what he had always wanted – to fit in and be like all the other kids. The kid who had been known by everyone as Johnny Strange transformed into Johnny Smooth. He flowed through social situations and navigated social rough spots with a smoothness that other kids came to admire. Johnny was incredibly happy with how things had changed for him.

The Calling to Be a Social Detective

But as fitting in became more of a normal part of his life, Johnny started to realize something else. He began to realize that there was a reason why he had been different all those years. There was a reason why things had happened the way they did!

Most kids go through their lives never really thinking about social mysteries. They go through their lives never really thinking about why certain things work socially and other things don't. They just do what comes naturally. But for Johnny these things did not come naturally and, because of that, he had to work hard to understand what was going on socially.

Introduction

You could say the kids who never had to think about these things had it easy because they naturally fit in. They didn't have to worry about social problems all the time. But often, when those kids had problems, they didn't know how to deal with them. They didn't have the deeper understanding of social mysteries that comes from really having to think about your social world.

Johnny became an expert at solving social mysteries. And he knew that he could not let this new gift go unused. He felt an obligation to those less fortunate, those who were unable to solve their own social mysteries.

In the beginning, all Johnny had wanted was to fit in and not be Johnny Strange. But in time he realized that his destiny involved something much bigger. His destiny was bigger than earning the title of Johnny Smooth. His destiny involved helping others by starting the first ever detective agency dedicated to solving social mysteries.

Johnny started small, offering his services to a select number of kids who desperately needed his help. But before long, the news of what he was doing spread, and he became somewhat legendary at schools and neighborhoods far and wide. Kids from all over, and even adults, would come to Johnny and ask him if he would help them with their social mysteries.

The stories that follow are real cases taken from Johnny's detective journal. While the cases are real, the names have been changed to protect the innocent.

As you follow Johnny on his cases, see if you can solve the mysteries yourself. Following Johnny's steps for solving social mysteries will help you figure out the cases. You can use the "Procedures for Solving Social Mysteries Checklist" to guide you in your detective work.

Procedures for Solving Social Mysteries Checklist

Gathering the Facts

☐ Collect all the facts and write them down.

☐ Keep your eyes and ears open for clues.

☐ Pay good attention to what people say and how they say it. Pay good attention to what people say without words (i.e., body language and facial expressions).

☐ Always try to collect information about how other people see a situation.

☐ Look for clues in the surroundings and in events that happened before and after the social mystery.

☐ Always double-check to make sure you have your facts straight.

Making Sense of the Facts

☐ Break things down into pieces, in order to make whatever you are dealing with more manageable and easier to understand.

☐ Imagine how others might be seeing the situation: Put yourself in their shoes.

☐ Make sure to look at *all* the evidence.

☐ Go over the evidence many times, and try to see things from as many different points of view as possible.

☐ Discuss what you have found with other people in order to get fresh perspectives.

Creating Social Remedies

☐ Identify the problem.

☐ Identify what caused the problem.

☐ Brainstorm many different remedies to solve the problem. Be creative.

☐ Pick the top three remedies to test.

☐ Think about the pros and cons of each potential remedy.

☐ Test your top remedies one at a time.

☐ Take notes about any positive or negative side effects of your remedy to see how successful it was.

☐ If your remedy was not perfect, see if you can learn from it, and use the facts that came from it to create a new remedy.

Chapter 1

Too Close for Comfort: The Case of Back-Away Bobby

It was Tuesday, and I was finishing up my lunch in my usual spot in the cafeteria – third bench on the right, just past the vending machines. As I chewed, I wondered if the universe had been caught in some sort of glitch that made the same peanut-butter-and-jelly sandwich reappear in my lunch bag day after day. For the last week and a half, peanut butter and jelly on whole-wheat bread was the only thing my mother seemed to be doling out. I did love my PB and Js, but there was something called "too much of a good thing. "

Just as I washed down the last peanutty morsel, Antonio Closeupeenee approached. He stormed right up to me and stared straight into my eyes. I could feel the heat of Antonio's breath as he tried to find his words. Finally, after a long pause and lots of staring, Antonio spoke.

"I've had it with Bobby," he said. "I just can't take him any more."

I sat back in my seat and sized up Antonio. He was a big kid with lots of energy. When he moved, he seemed to create a sort of vortex of motion around him. It was kind of like the feeling you get when a huge truck speeds by on the road and everything seems to shake a little.

After a moment of taking Antonio in, I asked him to go on.

"Bobby keeps saying he's my friend," he continued. "But every time we're playing with each other, he tries to run away from me."

"He runs away?" I asked, feeling my eyebrows rise to emphasize my question.

"Well, he doesn't really run," Antonio explained. "He just sorta keeps backing up. It's like he's always moving away from me, and a lot of the time when we're playing, he makes up some excuse why he has to leave and then goes away. Sometimes he'll get up and go after just a few minutes. And he's always telling me to get away from him. I'm sorry, but that's just not the way a friend should treat another friend."

Antonio's eyes were wide open, and his eyebrows were raised in a way that made it seem like they were both pointing directly at the crinkle he was making on his forehead. You didn't have to be a social detective to figure out that he was extremely upset.

"I can't understand how someone who is supposed to be my friend could be so mean to me," Antonio said, wringing his hands.

I listened carefully to Antonio's story. When he was done, I asked him to give it to me again from the top. I often ask people to repeat things to make sure I get all the facts straight. Because trying to solve a mystery without getting the facts straight is like trying to pee in the dark. There is a good chance you're gonna miss and make a mess of things, if you know what I mean. Anyway, when Antonio finished telling me his story for the second time, I could tell he felt a little calmer.

I had seen Bobby and Antonio together before, and they did seem to be good friends. But what Antonio was describing did not sound friendly at all. There was definitely a mystery to be solved here.

"I'll take the case, Antonio. The cost is a dollar a day plus expenses."

Antonio agreed to the terms, and I told him I would start right away.

"So what should I do, Johnny?"

"Just go about things as usual, Antonio. What are your plans for today?"

"Bobby and I usually play on the playground after school," he sighed, then continued. "But I was thinking that maybe I should take a little break from playing with him since it seems that he doesn't really want to be my friend."

"Let's not assume anything, Antonio," I said. "One possibility is that he doesn't want to be your friend any more, but there are other possibilities. A good social detective always tries to think of alternative reasons for things before coming to conclusions.

"And besides that," I added, "I've seen you and Bobby together, and it seems like he likes you. I mean, he's told you he's your friend before, hasn't he?"

"Yeah, I guess so," Antonio replied, taking a deep breath.

"Okay then. Just do what you usually do for the rest of the day, and we will figure out this mystery, alright?"

Antonio nodded.

The afternoon seemed to last forever. Science was my last class that day, and Mrs. Dullard was telling us something about gravity. As she talked, I could feel the powerful force of gravity pulling down on my eyelids.

Science is actually one of my favorite subjects, but Mrs. Dullard has a unique talent for making even the most interesting things boring. Her monotonous voice and robot-like body language have a hypnotic effect that seems to command even the most enthusiastic science lover's eyelids to get heavy. She also seems to have an almost magical ability to slow down time. I swear, when I watch the second hand on the clock in her class, it repeatedly stops for long periods of time without any forward movement whatsoever. As a result, seconds seem like minutes, and minutes seem like days.

My way to combat Mrs. Dullard's hypnotizing spell is to let my mind wander. I am really good at science so I can afford a little wandering in her class. And today my mind was wandering to Antonio and his situation.

Why would Bobby do what he was doing? Was Antonio reading the situation correctly? Was there something else going on that Antonio was somehow not aware of? These were all important questions, and I wrote them down in my case notebook. But to answer them, I needed more information. I needed to get the facts straight.

After school, I positioned myself behind the big oak tree at the end of the playground so I would not be seen by Antonio or Bobby. As always, I had my notebook ready for writing down clues and leads. For this case, I also employed the services of my binoculars so I could see close up without anyone knowing I was there.

The playground was alive with the excitement of the school day ending. Some kids were playing kickball while others were jumping rope. The handball line was growing as more and more kids poured onto the playground for their much-needed dose of after-school entertainment.

Bobby was at the monkey bars when Antonio approached. Antonio came right up to Bobby and put his hands on his shoulders. Bobby turned and cracked a smile. He seemed happy to see Antonio. The boys started monkeying around just the way you're supposed to on monkey bars.

I couldn't hear what Bobby and Antonio were saying, but the looks on their faces and the bounce in their steps made it clear that they were having a good time together. Antonio jumped towards Bobby and bumped him with his chest. Then Bobby started swinging on the bars and Antonio grabbed his legs and started pulling him. Bobby wrestled free and kept swinging. You could tell Antonio was really excited, but Bobby's mood was clearly changing. He wasn't smiling as much as he had been in the beginning.

I wrote some notes in my notebook. When I looked back up, Antonio was swinging on the bars beside Bobby, and in one quick lurching motion he wrapped his legs around Bobby and started shaking him and laughing. Bobby pulled free. Antonio dropped to the ground, and as he did I could see Bobby doing exactly what Antonio was saying he did. He was backing away.

The Case of Back-Away Bobby

Antonio would move closer to Bobby, and Bobby would back away. It seemed that the more Bobby backed away, the more Antonio would move towards him. And the more Antonio moved towards him, the more Bobby would back away. During this whole moving-towards and moving-away dance, Antonio seemed to be getting more and more excited, while Bobby was getting more and more irritated.

Within a minute of doing this dance, Bobby gave Antonio a quick wave and ran off towards the other end of the playground. Antonio was motionless, looking at Bobby as he disappeared into the distance. Slowly Antonio's forehead began to crinkle the way it had done when we were talking at lunch, and his eyebrows once again aimed themselves at that deepening crevasse forming on his brow.

Through my binoculars I could see Antonio's lips moving; he was saying something to himself. I couldn't hear what he was saying, but his body language said it all. His pained facial expression spoke loudly, alongside his hunching shoulders and hands that seemed to be wrestling with one another, all telling the tale of a very unhappy camper.

At that point, I put my binoculars away and turned my attention back to my notebook to finish writing down what I had seen. I had gathered all the facts I needed. I didn't need to see any more. It was clear to me what the problem was.

Can You Solve the Mystery of Back-Away Bobby?

Here are some questions that might help you in solving the case:

- How would you describe the mystery?

- What does Antonio see as the problem?

- What are the facts in this case?

- What are the biggest clues?

- How would you make sense of the facts?

- What do you imagine Bobby sees as the problem?

- Why do you think Bobby's mood changes during their playing?

- Why do you think Bobby finally stops playing with Antonio?

- What do you imagine Johnny thinks the problem is?

- Do you think you would be friends with Antonio? Why?

- What social remedies would you offer to Antonio?

- How would you test out your social remedies to see if they were working?

Cracking the Case

I had just finished documenting my playground surveillance in my notebook when I felt the vortex of motion moving towards me. It was Antonio. He had spotted me by the tree and was quickly moving in my direction. He ran up and placed his hands on my shoulders.

"Did you see, did you see what he did?" Antonio cried out. "Why is Bobby acting that way, Johnny? Why doesn't he want to be my friend? Can you help me solve the mystery? Can you?"

"I think the answer to your mystery is clear," I said, gently taking Antonio's hands off my shoulders and moving back a few steps. "The mystery is really not a mystery at all. This is clearly a case of personal space."

I paused for a moment to let my words sink in. I also paused because I rather enjoyed my little rhyme – "clearly a case of personal space." It seemed like a cool detectivey thing to say. But I could tell by the blank look on Antonio's face that he was not in the right frame of mind to enjoy my rhyme, so I moved on.

"The evidence has been there all along, Antonio. From what I observed, Bobby really did seem excited to see you when he arrived. It was clear by the look on his face that he was happy you were there. And when the two of you started playing, his body movements were bouncy, and he was facing you and interacting with you really nicely."

"I was excited to play with Bobby, too," Antonio said.

"I could tell that as well. But the way you express your excitement and enthusiasm is different than the way Bobby does. Do you know how you express your enthusiasm?" I asked.

"Uhh, I get happy."

"I'm sure that's true, Antonio. But do you know how your body expresses it?"

"Well ... uhh, I guess I ... Mmm ... I guess I don't really know."

"It seems clear to me that when you're excited, like you were when you and Bobby were playing, you express it in a very physical way. You express it by moving around with a lot of energy, and you express it with physical contact."

"Yeah, that makes sense," Antonio said. "I do have a lot of energy. People tell me that all the time."

"Energy can be a great thing. But it's important to know how to manage your energy and how other people respond to it, because it can be overwhelming to other people.

The Case of Back-Away Bobby

"When you got excited," I continued, "you started moving more and more into Bobby's personal space. And the more excited you got, the less excited Bobby got. The more you moved into his space, the more he would back away from you. It seemed that the more he would back away, the more you would try to get even closer to him, which made him back away even more."

"I didn't notice that," said Antonio, "but I guess, in thinking back, I can kind of see it."

"I suspect that when Bobby tells you to get away, he is not saying he doesn't want to play with you, Antonio. I suspect he is saying that you are too close to him physically. And it makes perfect sense that when you don't respond to his request for some personal space, he gets frustrated and leaves. People like it when we respond to their needs, and they get frustrated and often don't want to play with us when we don't."

"I don't want Bobby to be mad at me, but sometimes when I'm having fun, I don't really think a lot about things."

"Maybe you can start thinking more about those kinds of things, Antonio," I suggested.

"That sounds like a good idea. I'm just not sure how to do it, Johnny."

"There are some pretty simple things you can do," I said reassuringly. "First, it's important that you remember that this is a case of personal space. You've gotten a very important lead today. The lead is that sometimes you have trouble with personal space. If you remember this when you're with people, it will help you to notice if you are too close.

"Another thing that's really important," I added, "is to always be on the lookout for clues. A good friend always looks for clues about how people are responding to him. He looks for feedback about how he's acting and adjusts his actions accordingly.

"Bobby gave you some really good clues. First, he said, 'Get away.' That's a pretty big clue. Next, he kept backing away from you. This is another good clue that you were too close. His mood also changed as you got more and more excited, and as you moved more and more into his personal space.

"Sometimes we miss clues that are right in front of us," I continued. "When that happens, people's actions seem like a mystery to us. But if you remember that the way people act towards us usually holds some clues about our own behavior, it will help you to see things clearer. And now that you know that this is a case of personal space, it will help you notice more when people may be giving you feedback that you are too close to them."

Antonio looked puzzled. "So how far away from people should I stay?"

The Case of Back-Away Bobby

"It depends on the situation and on the person, Antonio. When a kid is snuggling with his mom or dad, there is not much personal space between them. But if that same kid is in a fight with his parents, I imagine there would be a lot more personal space.

"Usually with friends there is a certain amount of personal space even when we are getting along really well. A basic guideline would be to make sure you are at least an arm's length away from someone when you are playing. Of course, there will be times when you are sitting right next to someone with no space in between, and times when you are far away from each other. The key is to think about what seems best in the situation you are in, and to remember to be aware of the clues the other person is giving you."

Antonio seemed relieved. "You rock, Johnny," he said as he moved in close to me. He reached his arm forward but then caught himself. "Personal space ... Gotta watch my personal space."

I slapped his hand with mine. "High five, buddy! You're a quick learner. I think it's safe to say that this mystery is solved!"

Chapter 2

Accidentally Funny: The Case of the Incidental Straightman

It was Wednesday morning, and the weather outside was perfect. Sunlit clouds speckled a deep blue sky, and a gentle wind inspired the treetops to dance. It was the kind of weather that made even the most serious kid daydream about all the things he could be doing, if he were only on the other side of that big classroom window.

I was sitting in math learning about numbers and all the things they can do, when the kid next to me started talking. His name is Dimsly Overhead. At first I didn't realize Dimsly was talking to me. His voice was quiet, and he was staring at the floor.

"I don't get it," he mumbled. "I don't get what's so funny about me. I just don't get it. Do you have any idea what might be so funny?"

I looked around to see if there was someone else he might be talking to. There was no one.

"Are you talking to me?" I whispered, trying to stay undetected by teacher radar.

"Yeah, Johnny. Yeah, I wanna know what you think about it," he said in a mumbly voice.

"Dimsly … what on earth are you talking about?" I asked.

"You know. Kids always think I'm funny, but I'm not sure why. I mean, I'm not trying to be funny. And I don't really think I'm all that funny. But they all seem to think I am. You're the detective, right? So can you detective me, or something?"

I was intrigued. "Accidentally funny." That definitely sounded like a mystery. I told Dimsly to meet me after class to discuss the case further. I didn't think that Mrs. Krabington would appreciate us solving social mysteries while she was trying to help us solve number mysteries. There was a reason she had the nickname "The Krabinator," and the last place anyone would want to be was in the line of fire of her krabinicious krabittude.

Eventually, math ended, and I followed the flow of kids out of class. Dimsly strolled slowly and somewhat aimlessly down the hall, which made it easy for me to join up with him. I tapped him on the shoulder and smiled.

The Case of the Incidental Straightman

"Hey, Johnny," he said, and then paused, seeming to have forgotten our conversation in class. Then I could see the light go on. "Oh yeah, you're gonna detective me, right?"

Dimsly was a small boy with blond hair and gray blue eyes that always seemed to have a slightly glazed, dozing quality to them. He had a sweet smile and a gentle manner, but the thing that stood out most was the unwaveringly confused slant of his eyebrows that gave one the very strong sense that Dimsly had absolutely no idea of where he was.

"I'd like to hear a little more about your case before I say for sure that I'm going to take it," I answered. I took out my notebook. "Okay, Dimsly, give me the facts."

"Well, Johnny, I seem to be funny or something. I'll be having a conversation, you know, just talking like kids do, and out of the blue, right in the middle of my saying something serious, the other kids start laughing. It's really weird. And when I ask them what was so funny, they laugh even more. They just keep laughing and laughing, and sometimes I get so frustrated that I end up storming off."

"That does sound like a mystery to me, Dimsly," I agreed. "You really have no idea why they might be laughing?"

Dimsly paused and looked at me. His face looked confused, but it was hard to tell if it was the confused look he usually had or something more.

"They're laughing because they think I'm funny," he said.

"Yeah, yeah, I know that part. But do you have any idea why they think you're funny?"

My question was met with another pause and another confused look. After a few seconds, Dimsly smiled and shrugged his shoulders, letting me know without any words that he really had no clue.

"I'll take the case," I told Dimsly. I explained the deal like I always do: A dollar a day plus expenses.

Dimsly agreed, although that permanently confused look on his face made me repeat what I had said just to make sure he got it.

He agreed again. I told him to go about his day, and I would be on the case. That afternoon was the school health fair, and there was a party for all the kids during fifth period. That would be the perfect opportunity to watch Dimsly in action.

Wednesday, 1:30 PM

I arrived at the party a few minutes late so that I could get a feel of the layout after all the kids were already there. I thought that would help me figure out the best place to gather clues.

The Case of the Incidental Straightman

For a social detective, scouting out the layout is not just about seeing how things like tables and chairs are set up. It is about seeing how people are set up and are interacting with each other.

How were the people broken up into groups? What were the groups talking about? What was the mood of the people? What was my relationship like with all the people in the different groups? These are some of the types of questions good social detectives need to ask in order to truly understand the social layout of a situation.

The physical layout of the party was pretty basic. There were rows of tables with pamphlets about healthy eating and exercise and things like that for the kids. There were also some grown-ups talking to the occasional kid who actually went up to the tables. They would tell them about all the things they could do to be healthy.

At the other end of the room were tables filled with healthy refreshments – nuts, fruit, vegetables and juice. The most interesting snack, and the one that generated the most conversation among the kids, was green crackers made from seaweed. I filled my plate with a little of everything. Everything except the strange-smelling seaweed crackers. Frankly, they scared me.

Even though there were groups of chairs set up for the party, most of the kids were standing. After assessing the physical setup, I turned my attention to the social layout.

Groups of kids were scattered around the room. Some groups were engaged in lively conversation, where there seemed to be no space between people's comments back and forth. Other groups seemed more chilled out in their style of talking, with pauses in the conversation. Sometimes those types of conversations are easier to join in because there is room left in the conversation to say something.

Then I spotted Dimsly. As luck had it, he was standing with a group of kids I knew from math class. I walked up and placed myself at the edge of the group in order to join in. That way I did not disrupt the conversation, but at the same time, I made it clear that I had arrived and wanted to be a part.

"Hey, Johnny," Amanda said.

"Hey, Amanda. How's it going?"

We all chatted about this and that, joking about health food, teachers' personalities and where on earth someone had come up with the idea of making crackers out of seaweed. Dimsly didn't say much but smiled a lot while we were all talking.

Then Joey looked at me and said, "So, Johnny …" He paused and then shifted his glance from person to person in the group, trying to get everyone's attention and making sure they were all listening to what he was about to say.

"So, Johnny," he said again. "What's up with you and

The Case of the Incidental Straightman

Krabington? Are you like the biggest teacher's pet ever?" He smiled mischievously and looked around again to make sure everyone else heard him.

Joey was bagging on me, as we call it at my school. He was challenging me to a verbal wrestling match. Joey was a friend of mine, so I knew he was being playful, in that sort of mean way boys often play with each other. But it was a challenge to wrestle just the same.

I looked Joey straight in the eyes and paused for a moment without blinking. This gave me a little time to decide on the best strategy for responding. I could defend. I could attack back. I could say nothing. I could laugh it off with no real response. Or I could "work it," as I like to call it. That means taking something that could be to your disadvantage, turning it around and using it to your advantage.

I decided to work it. I put on my most serious face and sighed, "Joey, you found out my secret. I'm ..." I paused for dramatic effect and continued. "I'm ... in love with the Krabinator."

All the kids laughed. All but Dimsly! His smile faded, and his face took on a look of distress. "She's old enough to be your mother, Johnny!" he blurted out. All the other kids started laughing even louder.

I continued shifting my eye contact from Joey to the other kids, in order to make sure they were all still with me, and to keep them engaged by letting them know I was paying attention to them.

"You see, the Krabinator and I are going to get married and have lots of little Krabs, and they are going to take over the school and torture all the kids with pink slips and detention and extra homework every night." I let out an evil laugh, and all the kids burst out laughing again. All but Dimsly.

Dimsly's face, which was first smiley then confused, was now the face of someone completely freaked out. "Stop it, Johnny," he said. "You're gonna give me nightmares!"

The other kids roared with laughter. They thought Dimsly was hilarious, and of course they were right. He was hilarious. But they were also dead wrong. I didn't need any more information. This mystery was solved.

 # Can You Solve the Mystery of the Incidental Straightman?

Here are some questions that might help you in solving the case:

- How would you describe the mystery?

- What does Dimsly see as the problem?

- What are the facts in this case?

- What are the biggest clues?

- How would you make sense of the facts?

- How do you imagine the other kids saw the situation?

- Why do you think the other kids laughed at Dimsly's comments?

- What do you imagine Johnny thinks the problem is?

- Why did Johnny say the kids were both right and wrong about Dimsly being hilarious?

- Do you think you would be friends with Dimsly? Why?

- What social remedies would you offer to Dimsly?

- How would you test out your social remedies to see if they were working?

 **Cracking the Case**

As the laughter died down a little, the conversation took a natural turn. We had spent just the right amount of time talking about the Krabinator, and now it was time to move on to other topics like who in their right mind would choose to eat seaweed crackers.

The change in conversation topics was my opportunity to transition smoothly out of the group. I tapped Dimsly's shoulder, made eye contact with him and motioned for him to come with me. He still looked freaked out and confused.

We walked over to one of the unoccupied tables and sat down.

"Did you really think I was in love with Mrs. Krabington?" I asked.

Dimsly just stared at me with his trademark slightly confused look, and then after a long pause, he shrugged his shoulders.

"Any idea why the kids were laughing in response to the things you said?" I asked.

"They thought I was funny?" Dimsly replied. "But I'm still not sure why."

"Well, I think the answer to your mystery is clear, Dimsly. Let me explain. When you said Mrs. Krabington was old enough to be my mother, or that I was going to give you nightmares, the others kids thought you were joking. They thought you knew I was joking, and that by pretending to take me seriously you were joking about my joking. It's called **irony**."

"Ironing, like you do with clothes?" Dimsly probed.

"That's funny, Dimsly. But I don't think you meant to be funny.

The Case of the Incidental Straightman

When someone is using irony, they are saying something that is different than what they really mean. The other kids thought you were being ironic because they didn't really think you believed me. They thought you knew I was joking and that you were joking back with me."

"How do I tell whether someone is joking or not?" asked Dimsly with a very serious face.

"That's a great question, Dimsly, and one that I think gets to the heart of your mystery. The first step in solving that kind of puzzle is to remember that people are not always being literal. To be literal means to say exactly what you mean without any exaggeration or imagination to spice things up.

"But people often spice up what they say," I continued, "and, as a result, do not say exactly what they mean. They leave it up to the listener to put the puzzle pieces together and figure out what part of what they are saying is exactly right and what part is playful, or trying to express something else.

"Just like kids play on the playground, people play with words," I explained. "Sometimes kids pretend to be cops and robbers to have fun. And sometimes people play with words to have fun. Like me pretending to be in love with Mrs. Krabington. But people usually give off a lot of clues when they are being ironic or when they are not being literal. Clues might be a little smile on their face, rolling their eyes or a change in the tone of their voice."

"But when you were talking about Mrs. Krabington, you seemed really serious, Johnny."

"Good point, Dimsly. You see, the clues can be tricky. Sometimes the clues come from things that people share in common and about things people agree are realistic. So let me ask you this. When you really think about it, can you ever *realistically* imagine me and Mrs. Krabington being together, or us having babies with each other?"

Dimsly thought for a minute. "I guess when you ask me like that, and with what you just said about being ironic and literal … I guess that does not seem like the most realistic thing."

"That's great, Dimsly," I said encouragingly. "So when you are with people, your number one job as a social detective is to keep asking yourself if they are being literal or ironic. To help, just like any good detective would do, make a list of questions to ask yourself.

"Here are a few you can ask yourself: Are people being ironic? Are they being literal? Is what they are saying really realistic or are they playing with words and ideas? Are there any clues, like their facial expression or tone of voice, that might tell me they are not completely serious about what they are saying?

"Another great clue that could help you realize when people are joking rather than being serious is if they start laughing. If they start laughing at what you say, then try joking back and see what happens."

The Case of the Incidental Straightman

 "So you're not gonna marry the Krabinator, then?" Dimsly asked.

I looked at him, wondering if he had heard anything I had just explained.

Then he cracked a smile and said, "How was that for irony?"

We both laughed. "Nice job, Dimsly. I think this case is officially cracked."

Chapter 3

Summer's Bummer: The Case of the Huffy Girlfriends

Her name was Summer McLouden, and she was beautiful. Long brown hair with eyes that made you feel right at home. She was the kind of girl you could easily imagine a young boy getting big in the heart over. But the facts were that no one seemed to like her much.

"Johnny, Johnny, I need your help bad!" Summer announced as she leaned over the cafeteria table where I often set up my office at school. "My world is crumbling around me! The entire school seems to be repulsed by everything I say!"

I winced a little as Summer spoke. It was barely 10 o'clock in the morning, and Summer was taking my still sleepy brain by surprise. I put up my hand the way the crossing guard does when she is stopping traffic, took a deep breath, centered myself and then asked Summer to go on.

She explained how more and more her friends seemed to be getting irritated with her for no reason. They would tell her to stop talking and to leave them alone.

"Just this morning before school we were all sitting together, and suddenly Amy and Becky got up in a huff and left me all by myself!" Summer said by way of explanation.

Summer was very upset and needed my help. The class bell rang, marking the end of our morning snack time and the beginning of recess, and herds of kids began their migration out of the cafeteria. I told her how it worked, a dollar a day plus expenses. She agreed.

Tuesday, 10:32 AM

Good detectives always start with the facts, so I decided to begin my investigation right away during morning recess to see what clues I could find. A group of girls had gathered at the far end of the playground, jump ropes in hand. Summer, Becky and Amy were in the pack.

I sat down on the patch of grass right next to the jump rope area. It was the perfect spot to observe from. I realized that if I sat there all by myself and stared at the girls jumping rope, it would blow my cover. I'd probably also get a lot of strange looks from other kids thinking I was sitting there staring at the girls. A good social detective has to be aware of how others might be seeing him. In fact, that's true for anyone who wants to be good at being social, not just for us social detectives. So I pulled out a comic book, *Mega Man #27*, to be exact, and used it as my cover, peering over the top so no one would know what I was up to.

There was a murmur of excitement from the group of girls as they formed a line and decided on which song to sing while they jumped rope. The group consensus was "Ice Cream, Soda Pop, Cherry on the Top." They began to sing, and one by one the girls took their turns jumping over the spinning rope.

I watched and watched and listened, but nothing seemed that much out of the ordinary. Sometimes surveillance work can be a little slow. My mind started to drift as I observed the girls moving up and down and up and down, while chanting their rhythmic songs.

I imagined a tribe of warriors doing an ancient war dance in preparation for a big battle, but I was pretty sure that this was not how any of the girls were seeing things. Boys and girls often see things differently, and I always try to remember that so I can do my best to understand the ways girls see things.

The recess bell rang, and I was still without any leads. I needed more facts, so I planned a lunchtime surveillance.

Tuesday, 12:01 PM

I walked into the school cafeteria and set up at a table in the corner. My tools for this stake-out were my detective notebook for writing down clues and my detective listening device, which can pick up a whisper 200 feet away. I was close enough not to need binoculars for this surveillance; besides, that might look kind of strange in the cafeteria.

Summer and her friends strolled in and sat down at the table they always sat at. I covered my listening device with my *Mega Man #27* comic book. That way no one would know what I was up to. The girls began to talk back and forth about some TV shows they had all seen the night before.

Discreetly, so no one would notice, I adjusted the direction of my listening device so that I could tune in to Summer and her friends. As I was listening, a sharp pain soon pierced my ear and shot directly into my brain. The pain was the result of an incredibly loud sound screeching through my headphones.

I moved the headphones away from my ears so the sound was not as deafening. As I recovered from the shock, I realized that the piercing sound was Summer's voice! I had the volume set to pick up sounds at around 60 decibels, which is just about the volume of a normal conversation. But Summer's voice was much louder, and it almost blew out my earphones, not to mention my ear drums.

I could see the other girls wince when Summer talked. I also noticed something else that was very interesting. At the beginning of the conversation, the girls were all looking back and forth at each other pretty equally. They would shift their gazes to look at all the girls in the group when they were talking. Looking at someone when you are talking is a great way to keep them interested in you, and when you're talking in a group, giving everyone a little of your attention keeps them all with you.

I also noticed that when one girl was talking, all the other girls would be looking at her. Again, this was not out of the ordinary because that's one of the important ways in which a listener shows a speaker that they're interested in what they're saying.

But what was interesting was that as the conversation continued, the other girls started looking less at Summer when they were talking, and when Summer was the speaker they didn't seem to be looking at her at all. And it seemed that the less the other girls looked at Summer, the louder and faster she was talking.

I was getting a hunch, but I wanted to be completely sure. After all, Summer had paid me good money, and she was depending on me. So I planned one more surveillance, during library time that afternoon.

Tuesday, 1:32 PM

I walked into the library and immediately spotted Summer and her friends sitting at the round table in the back. That was the most sought-after spot in the entire library because it was the table located the farthest away from the librarian's desk. Not only was it far away, it was also around the corner and out of sight from any adults. It was the perfect place *not* to do your work, if you know what I mean.

Diary of a Social Detective

I went over and sat down at a small, one-person desk just behind Summer and her friends, with my back to the group. This time I had brought a special tool to test out my hunch. It was a sound meter, which measures how loud something is. You measure sound in decibels, and the louder something is, the more decibels show on the sound meter.

This time I used my history book as cover. After all, the library was for doing school work and while *Mega Man* was much more enjoyable than history, it was not really appropriate for the situation I was in. I pretended to read while pointing the sound meter microphone towards the group of chattering girls.

Their conversation was mostly gossip about other kids and secret crushes and what they thought the teachers were like outside of school. The sound meter readings were all around 50 decibels, which made sense. As mentioned, normal conversation is around 60 decibels, but the girls were in the library and trying to keep it cool and not get caught talking, so their voices were lower.

Amy began to talk, 30 decibels, almost a whisper. "You know who's really cute?" she asked. "Daniel."

There was a chorus of soft giggles, 40 decibels.

Then the sound meter spiked up to 80 decibels. "Daniel Buffington?" Summer blurted out.

"Shhh, yeah; Danny B," Amy said in response.

The Case of the Huffy Girlfriends

"That is so cool! Does he know you like him?" The sound meter hit 80 decibels again.

"No," said Amy. "And I'm trying to keep it that way."

"Your secret is safe here," Summer reassured her. "You and Daniel would make such a cute couple!"

You could tell Summer was happy for her friend, and her excitement shot the sound meter all the way up to 85 decibels. As decibels go, that is almost as loud as the sound of a lawnmower.

Amy got up and stormed off, followed by Becky. I turned around as Amy and Becky disappeared around the corner. Summer saw me and came over.

"Did you see that?" Johnny, she cried. "Did you? They did it again! What's wrong with my friends? I was really happy for Amy, and then she just got up in a huff and went away!"

I couldn't see my sound meter right then, but as Summer spoke, the image of a lawnmower was stuck in my mind. I told her to meet me after school so we could talk. She agreed.

I finished writing in my notebook, marking all the decibel readings I had just taken. The mystery was solved. No doubt about it.

Can You Solve the Mystery of the Huffy Girlfriends?

Here are some questions that might help you in solving the case:

- How would you describe the mystery?

- What does Summer see as the problem?

- What are the facts in this case?

- What are the biggest clues?

- Why did Summer's friends wince when she talked?

- Why were Summer's friends looking at her less and less as the group conversation progressed?

- What do you think Amy was feeling when Summer talked in a loud voice about her liking Daniel?

- How would you make sense of the facts?

- How do you imagine the other kids saw the situation?

- What do you imagine Johnny thinks the problem is?

- What do you imagine Johnny tells Summer when he meets her after school?

- Do you think you would be friends with Summer? Why?

- What social remedies would you offer to Summer?

- How would you test out your social remedies to see if they were working?

 ## Cracking the Case

My watch read 3:16 PM when Summer approached. It's true that sometimes a picture can say what a thousand words cannot. In this case, Summer's body language said it all! She was not a happy camper. Her shoulders were hunched as she slowly moved towards me, and her usually warm, inviting eyes had transformed into the biggest, saddest puppy-dog eyes I've ever seen.

Summer is not a bad kid. She has a big heart. But anyone who saw her could tell that her big heart was very heavy at that moment. I fought the urge to give her a hug. After all, I was a detective. This was professional, and I didn't want anyone to think I had some kind of crush on her. That would be ridiculous. I mean there would be no reason for anyone to think something like that, right?

Anyway, this was about Summer, and she needed my help. I snapped back into detective mode as Summer came to a stop in front of me.

"My friends hate me, Johnny," she started. "I try to be a good, supportive, loyal friend, but they just hate me."

I gave Summer a sympathetic smile instead of a hug. "You are a good, supportive and loyal friend, Summer. And it is clear that you have a big, kind heart."

"Maybe my heart is too big," Summer responded, "because it's making me feel really bad right now."

"It's not your big heart that's the problem, Summer. It's your big voice."

Summer's puppy-dog eyes widened, and her eyebrows raised just enough to give her face that questioning look people get when they want more information about something.

I continued. "Summer, do you ever notice that sometimes when you talk, people wince and even jump a little?"

"Not really," she replied.

"They do," I said in my nicest voice, not wanting to make her puppy-dog eyes get any bigger. "And the reason they do is that you frequently talk very loudly. Sometimes talking loudly isn't a problem. When you were playing jump rope with your friends on the playground, your loud voice fit in fine. Play-grounds are an appropriate place to be loud. No one winced then, and you seemed to get along great with your friends.

The Case of the Huffy Girlfriends

But when you were at lunch and were talking with the same uh … gusto, it was too loud."

Summer looked thoughtful. "What's the difference between the playground and the cafeteria, Johnny?" she asked.

"That's a good question. And the answer is that different situations call for different volumes. If you were to whisper on the playground when there was a lot of noise all around you, no one would be able to hear you. It wouldn't be appropriate to whisper there. Or if your friend just told you she won a million dollars and you whispered 'congratulations,' that would not fit the situation.

"In that situation a loud voice would express your excitement for your friend while a whisper might give your friend the impression that you did not really care about her good fortune. But whispering would be appropriate in, say, a library.

"Which brings me to what happened in the library today," I continued. "While playgrounds are a place for loud, exuberant voices and cafeterias are places for normal conversational voices, libraries are definitely places for whispers. And a library is even more of a place for whispers when you don't want the librarian to know you are not doing your work. And it is even more of a place for whispers when you want to make sure no one knows your friend has a crush on Daniel Buffington."

"You heard about Amy and Daniel?" Summer asked.

"Yes. I heard it from you, Summer. I think everyone in the library heard. That's why Amy got mad at you."

Summer's eyebrows rose. "But I was so excited for her. You just said that a loud voice lets someone know you are excited for them, Johnny."

"It's true that your voice can express excitement, but it's not as simple as that. There are many things to take into consideration when deciding how loud our voice should be. While excitement is one thing, the setting, in this case the library, is another.

"And then there is also the privacy factor of what you are talking about. Amy liking Daniel has a very high privacy factor for her. Because of that, it is something you must be very quiet about, in order to make sure you keep it private."

Summer paused and looked off into the distance. Her face was telling me she was thinking about what I had said and trying to take it in. I responded to what her face and body language were communicating and gave her a moment to think.

Eventually, her gaze returned to me. "How do I know how loud I am, Johnny?"

"That's a skill it may take some time to develop," I told her. "But I guarantee you that if you practice regularly, you will become more aware of what decibel you are talking at and what decibel level is appropriate for a given situation. The key is awareness.

"The first thing you can do is practice at home, deliberately talking loud and then talking in a whisper, and pay close attention to the differences. Practice different levels of loudness and see if you can notice the difference in how it feels in your throat and lungs, as well as how it feels to your ears at the different levels."

I pulled my handy decibel detector out of my pocket and handed it to Summer. "I'll also let you borrow this for a while if you like. It measures sound levels, and it tells you exactly how loudly you are talking. You can compare how loud you think you are with the detector's reading. Take it with you to different places and see how loud others are being in different situations. That will help you to get a better idea of what the appropriate sound level is in a variety of circumstances."

"You're so hi-tech, Johnny," Summer commented with a smile.

"Thanks, Summer." Our eyes met, and we paused for a moment. Sometimes it's the space between words that says the most. The pause in our talking slowed things down enough to let Summer's charm come out even more. It's amazing how much a voice that is too loud, or too fast, for that matter, can drown out all the other things that a person is trying to communicate.

I cleared my throat and looked down at my notebook to break our gaze. "Detective mode, Johnny," I reminded myself. Then I turned my gaze back to Summer.

"There is one last thing that I think will help you, Summer."

"What's that?" she said with a sweet smile on her face.

"If you can measure how people are responding to you, it will help you figure out if your voice volume is appropriate for a certain situation. I think it would be reasonable for you to assume that if someone is responding negatively to you, there is a fair chance it is because your sound volume is not matching what is called for in the situation."

"Do you have a fancy device for measuring that too, Johnny?"

I smiled. "Nope. There's no device for that, other than your own eyes and ears. But if you watch people's body language and listen to what they are saying and how they are saying it, you will get a lot of information."

Summer looked at me again and smiled. The sad puppy-dog gaze was gone, replaced by a warm twinkle. "Thanks for all your help, Johnny. I feel much better. How did you get to be so smart?" she asked.

I felt my insides get all mushy, and I was sure a blush was rapidly approaching. "It's not that big a deal," I said. "It's just practice. If you practice something long enough, what started out seeming difficult and hard to understand becomes simple and as natural as taking a breath of fresh air."

"I think this mystery is solved, Summer."

"I think so too, Johnny. Thank you for your help."

Summer gave me a hug and walked off. I took a deep breath. "Fresh air it was," I thought to myself. I loved being a social detective … for so many reasons.

Chapter 4

Gimme Back My Banana!: The Case of the Bothersome Bully

"Hey, Johnny, I have a question for you. Is part of a detective's job to be a bodyguard? If so, I want to hire you right away."

I lifted my gaze from the doodles in the margins of my history notes. While history class never really inspired me to learn more about the past, it frequently inspired me to develop my artistic abilities. And I have a whole notebook full of my doodled daydreams to show for it.

"Well, whatcha say, Johnny? Will you be my bodyguard?"

It was the Dupster. Stan Dupferself was his name, but for some reason he had gotten the nickname The Dupster. Or sometimes it was just Dup. What's up, Dup? was a greeting that frequently fell upon his ears.

With all the possibilities for nicknames and the potential for kids to be mean, Stan was blessed to have gotten a pretty neutral nickname. It was much better than my old nickname of Johnny the Strange.

Anyway, I looked up at Stan and, as I always do when dealing with people, tried to read him a little before responding – body language, facial expressions, things like that.

"Detectives and bodyguards are completely different things," I explained. "One's all brains and the other's all brawn, if you know what I mean. But using your brains can often protect you just as well as, if not better than, brute force. What seems to be the problem, Dupster?"

"It's Billy again. I seem to be his target of the week. He's ruining my life! He calls me names, he pushes me and he takes my stuff and makes be beg so he'll give it back. And the other kids laugh when he does it. He's ruining my life, Johnny. I need a serious bodyguard."

Stan was referring to Billy Bullington, an up-and-coming tormentor of the weak, awkward and defenseless. Billy was new to the bully scene and, on the continuum of bullies, he was relatively harmless. While he might on occasion get a little physical with kids, he was never really violent or aggressive. And when push came to shove, Billy would usually back down.

The Case of the Bothersome Bully

Billy was what I like to call a "wannabe funny bully." This is the type of kid whose real goal is to get attention and look cool. He was the type of kid who would have liked to get positive attention, or even be an effective class clown, but was not able to accomplish either. So instead he resorted to getting laughs by humiliating others.

Billy was pretty much an open book, as bullies often are. But the real mystery here was how The Dupster got caught in Billy's line of fire. Billy usually picked on the kids who had no friends and were socially awkward. Stan seemed like a pretty cool kid and had lots of friends. So how did he get targeted by Billy?

This seemed like a genuine mystery to me, and good social mysteries are what I'm all about. So I told Stan I couldn't promise anything but that I would take the case if he wanted. I made it clear that there would be no bodyguarding but that I would help him figure out why this was happening and what he could do about it. "A dollar a day plus expenses," I said. He agreed.

Mr. Tolerento was well liked by the kids because of his kicked-back attitude, but Stan's and my whispering seemed to be going on a little too long for his liking. A clearing of the throat, a glance in our direction and a slight raising of the left eyebrow was all Mr. Tolerento had to do to let us know it was time to get back to business. We both turned our gazes back to our history notebooks. And it was just as well, because I wanted to finish my doodle before the bell rang.

Wednesday, 10:00 AM

I followed Stan out of class.

"Here you go, Johnny," Stan said as he handed me a dollar.

"Alright, Stan. Now just go about things as usual and don't stress too much. We'll figure it out."

Stan gave me a nod and walked toward his locker. I slowed my pace and let Stan move ahead. As luck – or rather bad luck – would have it, Billy was coming down the hall from the other direction, on what seemed to be a direct collision course with Stan.

I could see Billy's face as he walked down the hall. He appeared pretty low energy, with slightly hunched shoulders and a facial expression that conveyed a hint of loneliness, and maybe even sadness. But that all changed when he saw Stan. At the mere sight of his victim, Billy came to life. His body straightened up, and his face went from slightly sad to excited.

He sped up his pace to intercept Stan. My detective instincts told me it might come in handy to catch this exchange on tape, so I pulled out my newest detective tool. It was a small video recorder with a tiny remote lens and microphone that I could hold in my hand and point at whatever it was I wanted to record. This made it easy to video things without a lot of attention being drawn to me.

The Case of the Bothersome Bully

I should make it clear that using devices like this and listening devices and any type of spy device for that matter is usually against school policy and might even be against the law as far as I know. And most of all, these things could be used in ways that invade the privacy of others. It was only after countless cases and proving myself with the school faculty that the principal gave me special permission to use this kind of equipment for the sole purpose of solving social mysteries.

Anyway, I followed Billy with my new little toy as he moved close into Stan's personal space and began talking to him. "What's up, Dopster?" he said, mockingly. "Feeling Dopey today? Get it? Dopey, like dumb. What's up, dummy?"

Stan didn't say anything and just kept walking toward his locker.

"Hey, I'm talking to you, Dopster. You deaf or something?"

"Just leave me alone, Billy," Stan said in a whiney voice.

"And why should I leave you alone, Dopey?"

Stan's whole body seemed to hunch over in response to Billy. It was strange to see. Stan who is normally a pretty tall and athletic kid seemed to shrink a good two or three inches as Billy kept tormenting him. And Billy, who had been hunched over just moments before himself, now seemed much taller and energized.

My mind filled with images of monkeys in the wild. At that moment, Billy reminded me of some big hairy chimpanzee trying to convince the other chimps that he was the biggest, baddest monkey in town. I imagined Billy beating his chest and making some primal subhuman war cry in order to get all the other monkeys' attention and respect.

Stan opened his locker and grabbed a banana and a bag of chips and started heading for the cafeteria for snack break.

"Hey Dopster, I'm talking to you."

"Just leave me alone," Stan whined, as he attempted to walk around Billy.

"How about I take this, Dopey?" Billy said as he grabbed Stan's banana from his hand.

Stan let out a strange guttural cry and flapped his arms. The act of snatching Stan's banana paired with the image of Billy as some attention-seeking hairy monkey was too much, and I laughed out loud.

I wasn't laughing at Stan! I felt compassion for him. But the truth was that even though Billy seemed like a big jerk and I felt for Stan, the whole scene was funny in some strange way. Billy, like some primitive banana-grabbing monkey, and Stan flailing his arms and making strange sounds … Funny.

Other kids seemed to have the same reaction, and they started laughing as well. This made Stan shrink even more. Seeing Stan's reaction to the kids laughing snapped me out of the temporary spell I was under, and I quickly got back into detective mode.

Stan seemed to accept his loss of banana and stormed off fruit-less, so to speak. In the meantime, Billy smugly laughed to himself and looked to the kids who had been laughing. The other kids gave Billy no attention whatsoever; however, Billy seemed oblivious and proudly sauntered down the hall with his bright yellow trophy in hand. I continued to video the scene as Billy strutted off into the distance, but I really didn't need to see any more. The facts were all too clear.

Can You Solve the Mystery of the Bothersome Bully?

Here are some questions that might help you in solving the case:

- How would you describe the mystery?

- What does Stan see as the problem?

- What are the facts in this case?

- What are the biggest clues?

- Why do you think Billy got excited when he saw Stan?

- Why do you think Stan shrank two to three inches when Billy was teasing him?

- Why did Johnny and the other bystander kids laugh at what was happening between Stan and Billy?

- How would you make sense of the facts?

- How do you imagine the other kids saw the situation?

- What do you imagine Johnny thinks the problem is?

- What do you imagine Johnny told Stan when he met up with him later?

- Do you think you would be friends with Stan? Why?

- What social remedies would you offer to Stan?

- How would you test out your social remedies to see if they were working?

 **Cracking the Case**

Wednesday 10:09 AM

I caught up with Stan in the cafeteria and took him to my usual spot, third bench on the right, just past the vending machines. He was in bad shape. "Have a seat in my office," I said gesturing to the bench seat across from me.

The Case of the Bothersome Bully

I ripped off a piece of my fruit roll and put it in his hand. He accepted it and raised his eyes to meet mine as he brought my offering up to his mouth.

"I saw what happened, Stan. That was rough."

"I hate my life," he said with a twinge of whininess still in his voice.

"That was pretty bad, Stan. But it's definitely not hopeless from my point of view."

"Does that mean you're gonna be my bodyguard, Johnny?"

"Well, you do need a bodyguard. But there is only one guy who can really do the job."

"Yeah, who's that?"

"You, Stan. You. No one else can solve the problem. There's this old story about a boy and a fish. You see, the boy kept asking other people for a fish because he was hungry. People felt sorry for him, so they usually gave him a fish so he wouldn't be hungry any more.

"But one day the boy asked an old man for a fish, and the man said no. The boy couldn't understand why the man would say no. The old man had a huge pile of fish. The boy started walking away when the man called him back and told him that instead of giving him one fish, he was going to give him an endless supply of fish.

"And over the course of the next few weeks, the old man taught the boy all the secrets to fishing so the boy could catch as many fish as he wanted. Give a boy a fish, and he will only have a fish. And he will always be dependent on others to get his needs met. But teach a boy to fish, and he will have a lifetime of fish."

I looked at Stan with a grin on my face, expecting something like a "Cool story, Johnny. I get it – it all makes sense now" type of reaction. But instead, Stan just stared at me.

I raised my eyebrows a little to say, "So … what do you think; you get it?"

But Stan just stared back as if to say, "What the hell are you talking about, Johnny?"

"Okay, Stan; it's like this. If I were to somehow get Billy to lay off you that would just be like giving you a fish. That would not help you to deal with all the other Billys in the world.

"But if you can figure out how to be your own bodyguard, how to stand up for yourself, you will have a lifetime of fish, if you know what I mean."

"You mean I'll be able to deal with other jerky kids like Billy?" Stan asked.

The Case of the Bothersome Bully

"Exactly, Stan. Exactly."

"Alright, let's give it a try. At this point I'll try anything."

"Okay. The first thing you need to do to solve a social mystery like this is to gather all the facts. The facts are that Billy is playing you like an old violin."

Once again Stan just stared at me, and I read his expression to say, "Dude, how about speaking a little English here?"

"Sorry, Stan, I read that term in a detective book the other day and was dying to use it. Billy is 'playing you.' He's using you to try to get attention and feel good about himself, and you are going along without any resistance. You are an easy target for him because you just let him torment you without standing up for yourself."

"But aren't you supposed to ignore bullies, Johnny? That's what my mom always tells me to do." .

"Yeah, my mom tells me I look good in plaid pants and a bow tie, Stan. While she means well, she does not always understand the ins-and-outs of today's social world. And while your mom is correct in thinking that there is a time and a place for ignoring the bully, it is not always the case.

"The first thing you gotta do is size up your bully. Some bullies are really bad, and if you do anything but ignore them, you are asking for trouble. I call those kids 'the dangerous bullies.' Billy is not in that category. He is what I call 'a wannabe funny bully.' If you look at his history with other kids, he has never gotten violent, and he usually backs down if you challenge him."

"But he didn't back down with me, Johnny. I told him to stop and he kept harassing me."

"Well, the truth is, Stan, you didn't genuinely tell him to stop. Even though your words said stop, your voice and body language were not very forceful."

I played back the video-tape for Stan so he could see his interaction with Billy from a more objective point of view. I pointed out his hunched body language and whiney voice tone.

"Wow, Johnny. Is that how I came across?"

"I'm afraid so, Stan. But the reality is that's not how you usually come across. Somehow Billy throws you off balance, and he feeds on your reaction to him. And even though it may have seemed to you that you did what your mother told you to do and ignored him, when you really look at the facts, it's clear that you didn't ignore him. Had you ignored him, you wouldn't have showed him any reaction. But you gave him a lot of reaction. Even if you are having a reaction inside, you don't have to let him know it."

"That's impossible, Johnny," argued Stan. "How can I hide how he is making me feel?"

The Case of the Bothersome Bully

"Well, there are a couple of things you can do so bullies like Billy won't know they are getting to you. The first thing you can do is to just laugh a little when he makes his comments and then keep walking. Laughing gives the other person the impression that you are not taking them seriously. It also can help you to not let what they are saying get to you. Laughing helps us see the humor in things, and the more humor there is, the less likely we are to take what someone like Billy says too seriously.

"You can also respond with the classic 'whatever.' When you say 'whatever' in a situation like that, what you are really saying is 'What you say or do has very little importance to me, and I really don't care at all about you or your actions.' That's the last thing a bully like Billy wants.

"Another thing that would be very helpful would be to stay aware of your body language. Did you notice in the video how you hunched over and made very quick, jerky, agitated movements in response to Billy? If you stay mindful of your body's responses, you will be more capable of choosing how you respond on the outside.

"Being aware can help you to stand up tall and respond with slow, calm body motions rather than quick, jerky, agitated motions. You can also remind yourself to keep your voice calm when responding to bullies like Billy, rather than whining or showing with your voice that they are getting to you.

"I imagine that if you do these simple things with Billy, he will realize you are not gonna give him the reaction he is looking for, and he will eventually get bored and start looking for some other kid to take out his problems on. But if those things don't work, you may have to move to the next level beyond ignoring.

"And while your mother may not fully endorse it, you may have to open up a can of attitude and start shooting some snappy comebacks in Billy's direction. Snappy comebacks show others that you're not easy prey."

"But I'm no good at snappy comebacks, Johnny."

"It is true that doling out effective snappy comebacks is an art that one has to develop, but with practice I bet you'll do fine. And you can start off with a few planned snappy comebacks that work in a variety of situations. Here are a few of my favorites:

"*The turn around:* When someone insults you, you pretend you didn't hear them right and respond as if they were saying it about themselves. For example, when Billy says, 'You're dumb,' you could say, 'What … you said that you're dumb? Don't be so hard on yourself, Billy.' Then he says, 'No, you're dumb, Dupster.' And you respond with 'Well, maybe you are dumb, Billy, but that's O.K., brains aren't everything.'

"*The exposure:* This type of snappy comeback aims at exposing the bully's real motive, or at least implies some embarrassing motive for them bullying you. So when Billy or some oth-er bully insults you, you could say, 'You're just saying that to get attention. Do you really think that being a jerk is going to get people to like you? Because that's what you're really try-ing to do, isn't it – get people to like you?' Or you could say, 'Insults are the unintelligent man's way of trying to be funny. And I stress the word *trying*.'

"The retaliation: If the first two comebacks are not strong enough, you can throw an appropriate verbal retaliation in your bully's direction, in response to his insult. A verbal retali-ation is an insult that you give back to the bully. The trick here is not to be too mean or too soft. If you're too mean, you might get the person really worked up, which could lead to more problems. It could also get you into trouble. You also don't want to stoop to the bully's primitive level by being overly personal or mean.

"You want to come out of the situation without any question that you are the emotionally bigger and more mature person. At the same time, you want your response to have some bite to it, so the bully knows that there is going to be a cost for messing with you. A few of the more popular retaliations are things like 'You're a dork' or 'You're a jerk.' 'Get a life, loser' often works nicely as well. If you spend a little time listening around school, you will get a good idea about what the more popular, up-to-date retaliations are. My top five favorite retali-ations this week are 'spineless weasel,' 'jello brain,' 'cheese head,' 'bozo' and 'scaly-faced, fly-eaten lizard.'

"With all these snappy comebacks, Stan, it's important to remember that it's not just what you say but how you say it. You want to make sure that you respond with a voice tone that is strong but not so emotional that the bully thinks he is really getting you upset."

"But what if none of that works, Johnny?" asked Stan. "What do I do then?"

"Ahhh. The 'final straw' as I like to call it. The final straw is setting a clear, unmistakable boundary."

"You mean a boundary like a wall?" Stan asked.

"What I mean by a boundary, Stan, is something that separates you from someone else. It is something that makes it clear when and where the other person must stop. It's kind of like drawing a line in the dirt and telling someone not to step over it. The first phase of setting a boundary with a bully involves stating very clearly and firmly what has to change.

"Saying 'Stop,' 'Back off,' 'Get out of my face' are some ways of setting a clear verbal boundary. If that doesn't work, you need to move to phase two of boundary setting – letting the person know that if he doesn't stop right away, you're gonna tell and he is going to get into trouble."

"But isn't that tattle-taling? I don't want to be a fink."

The Case of the Bothersome Bully

"A bully would want you to believe that setting this kind of boundary is tattle-taling. But there is a big difference between a tattletale and someone who stands up for himself and does not allow others to continue harassing him without doing anything. Tattletales tell on others for things that have nothing to do with them. Telling on another kid for not paying attention in class when it has absolutely nothing to do with you is clearly tattle-taling. But telling on someone who is doing something that is directly affecting you, when you have tried to get him to stop, is not tattle-taling.

"In fact, setting a boundary by telling on someone, after trying to get him to stop by other means, is a sign of self-respect. It is a sign that you realize you do not deserve to be treated like that and that you are not going to take it. It is a sign that you know how to solve problems.

"Now, of course, the bully will try to tell you that you're being a snitch if you tell on him. That's his way of trying to keep in control and not have any consequences for his behavior. Bullies may try to shame you or embarrass you out of telling on them and making them take responsibility for their bullying behavior. But if they try to do that, you can just respond with another snappy comeback. You could say, 'I'm not a tattletale, I'm just giving you what you deserve.' Or you could say something like 'If you don't want to be told on, then get out of my face.' Or 'If you just think you can hassle me without paying the price, you're wrong.'"

Stan looked at me very seriously. Then he looked across the cafeteria towards the table where Billy was sitting by himself eating his kidnapped banana.

"You know what?" Stan said. "Billy is a jerk!"

"And his jerkiness really is about him and not about you, Stan. That's important to remember. Well, I think it's fair to say this mystery is solved."

Chapter 5

You Catch More Flies With Honey Than With Vinegar: The Case of Billy's Burst Bubble

Anyone watching would have had no idea from his words and actions that Billy Bullington was trying to get me to help him. In fact, had it not been for my detective training, I'd never have been able to see through Billy's misguided attempts to be cool. I'd never have realized that he might be ready to solve his social mystery. And it was a mystery that needed to be solved, for everybody's sake.

"Hey, Johnny, solve any mysteries lately?" Billy said in a sarcastic voice. "Think you could solve a real social mystery, not some stupid little problem like all the other kids come up with?"

I don't usually respond to people when they act like Billy was acting, so I just kept my eyes fixed on the brand-new issue of my *Mega Man* comic.

Billy moved closer and grabbed the comic book out of my hand. "How about you solve my mystery and I'll give you back your comic?"

He had crossed the line. Not just any line, mind you. He had crossed the *Mega Man* line. I stood up without saying a word and glared at him. My eyes felt like laser beams, and I could feel the muscles in my face contracting in just the right way to express my anger perfectly. I did not blink or say a word, but my body, face and laser-like glare were saying loads. Billy placed my magazine back on the table and started talking in a different voice.

"So you gonna help me or what?" he said.

"Why would I want to help you when you take my magazine and talk trash to me?"

"I'm just joking around, Johnny. Why does everyone always take things so seriously?"

"Joking around has to be funny to everybody involved. What you usually do is jerking around. You act like a mondo jerk and think it's funny. You think you're just joking, but everyone else just sees you as being sarcastic and mean."

The Case of Billy's Burst Bubble

"Sarcasm is funny, Johnny," Billy said defensively. "You just don't got no sense of humor."

"Sarcasm tries to get a laugh by cutting others down," I replied. "It's what people do who can't get a real laugh."

"Alright, alright, give me a break, will ya? Come on, Johnny, seriously, I need your help."

I stared at Billy without saying a word. I was trying to take him in while giving myself some time to let my irritation settle down.

Billy Bullington was about as annoying as a kid could get. Everything he did made you not want to help him. But as I looked at this scruffy, slightly disheveled little boy, I could see that there might be something underneath the annoying show he put on that was worth helping.

And he really did need my help. Maybe it was just wishful thinking. Maybe it was my overly generous heart. Maybe it was the fact that I could remember my own past and all the clumsy things I did to try and fit in. Maybe it was the rush I was feeling due to the fact that spring break would officially be starting in a few hours. Whatever it was, I decided to hear what this not-so-friendly neighborhood bullyman had to say.

"So tell me, then. What do you think your mystery is, Billy?"

I knew what the problem was. In fact, I could solve this case without getting up from my seat. But I wanted to hear how Billy saw it.

Billy's posture slumped for a moment, and his face softened as he thought. It was as if he had stopped acting, stopped pretending. But it was just a flash. Within the blink of an eye the softening was replaced with the tough guy.

"The problem is that kids can't take a joke," he finally said cockily. "And I think kids get jealous of me way too much. You know, they get jealous because I'm so funny. And I think they get jealous because, you know, I'm the leader a lot."

"You're the leader?" I asked, trying to keep myself from laughing.

"You know, I'm always in charge when I'm with other kids," Billy explained. "They're jealous, and I want you to solve the mystery of why they're so jealous of me."

I stared at Billy. Speechless. There really was a mystery here. It was the mystery of how Billy could be so absolutely unaware of the social world he lived in. How he could be so unaware of how other people saw him.

Just then the silence was broken by the sound of the bell. "Time for class, Billy," I said. "I'll talk to you later."

The Case of Billy's Burst Bubble

"So you're gonna take my case, then?"

"I'm gonna think about it," I said. "And if I do take it, it's a dollar a day up-front plus expenses."

Billy fumbled with some words, trying to say something, but I started walking away and was immediately swept up in the current of kids moving towards their classes.

"Saved by the bell," I thought to myself. I needed some time to think about how I was going to handle this one. "How do you help a kid who is so blind to how others see him? How do you help a kid like that get a clue? That's the real mystery here."

I sat down in science class pondering how one gets the blind to see, and wondering if this would be the case to finally stump me. I could not imagine anything that would break through to Billy.

But just then, as fate would have it, good old Stan Upferself sat down next to me and, in seeing his face, the answer hit my brain like lightning.

"Hey, Johnny," Stan said as he nodded his head and gave me a half smile. It was the head nod half-smile combo that was the perfect greeting for letting people know you were happy to see them while still retaining your cool attitude.

"Hey, Stan, I got a question for you," I blurted out, still charged with the flash of lightning and the solution that flash had given me to Billy's mystery.

I knew that by not allowing the time and space to acknowledge Stan by saying something like "I'm good. How are you?," I was giving him the message that my question was more important than seeing him was at that moment.

People like it when they come first. Fortunately, Stan and I have a good relationship, and there is a lot of history of me showing him that he is important to me. But still I try not to make a habit of that kind of greeting with people who I want to stay friends with. It's just not good for keeping friendships strong.

"Uh, yeah, okay, what's the question, Johnny?" Stan said, trying to keep up with my abrupt jump from greeting each other to me questioning him.

"This may sound strange, Stan, but can I show that video where Billy was harassing you to someone?"

"Are you serious?" he asked.

"I know, I know, it probably sounds strange, but I think it could help someone else solve his social mystery."

"I don't know, Johnny, it's a little embarrassing. Who do you want to show it to?"

The Case of Billy's Burst Bubble

"Well, I can't really tell you that. I mean, as a social detective it's my duty to protect the confidentiality of my clients."

"But you're asking me if you can break my confidentiality. That video is kind of vulnerable. You know what I mean?"

This was a tricky situation. I knew the tape could help Billy. If he could see how other kids saw him, it might help him to realize how jerky he can be. But I couldn't show Billy the video unless I got Stan's permission. That wouldn't be respecting Stan's privacy.

At the same time, though, I couldn't tell Stan that Billy was my client without breaking Billy's confidentiality. Tricky indeed.

Before I could think of anything to say to Stan, fate stepped in. At just that moment, while Stan sat there staring at me, waiting for me to say something, Billy burst through the classroom door, walked over to me and slapped a dollar bill down on my desk.

"So if you don't solve my mystery, do I get that back?" Billy asked.

"Go to class, Billy," I said as Mrs. Smith cleared her throat in Billy's direction, saying very clearly but without words, "You better get out of my class right now, Mr. Bullington."

"Go to class," I repeated.

"Uh … alright. I'll talk to you later," Billy said as he turned and walked out the door, intentionally bumping into three kids who were walking in.

I turned my attention back to Stan. He was in total shock. His mouth was open wide enough to eat a triple-decker burger from the local In-N-Out, and his eyes seemed like they were about to bulge out of his head.

The sight was so funny that I started to laugh. But I had to stop myself because I knew that the reason why Stan was making that face had nothing to do with humor.

"You're … you're helping Billy?" Stan asked. "Please don't tell me it's Billy you want to show the tape to."

I didn't say a word. I just smiled. It was a careful smile – sometimes a smile can mean a lot of different things.

It wasn't a "ha ha that's funny" smile. That would not have matched the mood of the situation or expressed what I was trying to convey. And it was not the "what's up" half-smile we frequently gave each other as part of our cool greeting.

This was more of a conspiratorial smile. It was a smile that was letting Stan in on the secret without telling him in words. I didn't tell him directly that it was Billy I wanted to show the tape to. My little smile said it all. And it really was Billy who had said it, so I didn't have to worry about breaking the detective code of confidentiality.

The Case of Billy's Burst Bubble

"Why on earth would you want to show Billy that tape?" Stan asked. "So he could laugh at me more? And even if there was some good reason to show it to him, why would I do anything to help that butt-munchin' Neanderthal? He's one of the most obnoxious, despised bullies in our school. And the worst part is that he doesn't even realize how much we all despise him."

Stan was getting worked up. I could see a freaky-looking vein starting to swell on the side of his head, and little beads of sweat were forming just above his eyebrows. Stan was starting to catch on fire.

I needed to find some way to cool him down quick, if I were to have any chance of showing Billy that video. But, as I tried to figure out how to help him cool down, my mind could only think of one strange, surreal thing – "butt-munchin' Neanderthal." The words kept repeating in my head. "Butt munchin Neanderthal. Butt munchin Neanderthal" over and over again. How do you argue with that, especially when it fits so perfectly?

I must have had a strange look on my face as I stared speechlessly at Stan.

"Well?" Stan said.

I exaggerated the somewhat strange look I felt was building on my face. I imagined it was a slightly deranged, confused and comical look. And I said to Stan in my best question-asking voice, the only thing I could think of at the time … "Butt-munchin' Neanderthal?"

He burst into laughter. Then I burst into laughter. Sometimes laughter is a powerful medicine.

"I gotta admit, Stan. You do know how to sum things up."

Stan relaxed a little. Our laughter seemed to have broken the tension.

The truth was, what Stan was saying made sense. Why should he help Billy? I couldn't deny how much of a jerk Billy was to people. To deny that would not only have been untrue, it would have made Stan angrier than he already was.

When people are upset about something, the worst thing you can do is try to talk them out of their feelings. This just makes them angrier. It can make them think that you don't understand what they are feeling. Sometimes the best thing is to acknowledge the truth in what they are saying and feeling.

"I can totally understand why you wouldn't want to help him, Stan. And I totally get how frustrating it is that he doesn't realize how much people despise him. But maybe it's time he found out."

"And I think that with my help and the help of that video," I added, "there is a chance of him finally getting the picture. And maybe somehow helping Billy could also help all the other kids that Billy bullies all the time. Kids who are not as capable of standing up for themselves as you are, Stan."

Stan stared at me. The freaky vein-popping thing on the side of his head was now completely gone, thank God! As he stared, his face clearly conveyed two things at the same time. It conveyed that he was genuinely disgusted by the mere mention of Billy Bullington's name, and it conveyed the message that he was thinking.

I could tell he was thinking about what I had said. The bell rang, and Mrs. Smith held up her three-dimensional model of the solar system.

"The earth takes 24 hours to spin completely around, marking the end of an entire day."

"Twenty-four hours," I thought to myself. Twenty-four hours from now I'll be on spring break. Then a full week of school-free heaven will be mine. And in just a few hours, I'll be at Samantha's party, eating cake and hanging out with my friends.

Halfway through class Stan handed me a note saying, "You can show him the tape if you think it will help."

I looked over and gave him the nod-half-smile combo, and Stan returned it. I was hopeful that if Billy could see himself and others in a clearer way, he would come to realize what everyone else already seemed to know.

Science was always a fun class for me, so the bell rang before I knew it. I walked to the door calculating the remaining time until spring break officially started: 58 minutes and 30 seconds.

I gave myself the smile-head nod combo, but it was no half smile. There were no other kids to try to impress with my cool, casual attitude, so I let a big old toothy grin rip as I walked down the hall.

Billy was waiting for me outside the building. "Why so happy, Johnny? You couldn't wait to see me again, is that it?" he said, laughing to himself. Actually, he spent a lot of time laughing to himself, because other kids didn't seem to share his sense of humor.

Now that Billy was a client, it made it a little easier not to get so irritated by his obnoxious way of interacting with people. But not much easier! One of the things I often do when other people's poor social skills get to me is to remind myself of the problems I used to have, and remember that underneath those obnoxious behaviors is someone who is usually struggling and in pain.

I think the fact that Billy asked me for help showed that somewhere under his rude exterior he knew that something wasn't working in his life. The fact that he was able to recognize that he needed help made me able to see that there was some hope for Billy.

"Okay, Billy," I said. "Here's the deal. I have the solution to your mystery, but there is something I need to get at home to show you."

"But don't you have to find clues and all that detective stuff to solve my case?"

"Billy, I had your case solved before you even realized you had a case."

"What's that supposed to mean? Are you psychic or something?"

"Never mind, Billy. I'll try to explain that later. I tell you what. Let's meet at four o'clock at the park. I have to be somewhere at five, so let's both try to be on time."

"You going to Samantha's party?" Billy asked.

It's always awkward when someone asks you if you are going to a party that you know they are not invited to. You don't want to lie and say "no," but at the same time you don't want to rub their face in it by sounding too excited or focusing on the fact that they were not invited.

"Yeah, I'm going," I said in a casual, matter-of-fact voice.

"She didn't invite me," Billy said, staring at the ground with a thoughtful, slightly pained expression on his face.

I don't think I'd ever seen a thoughtful look on Billy's face before. It caught me off guard.

"Does that bug you?" I asked, hoping to reach beneath the obnoxious social mask he usually wears.

His face tightened a little but did not go back to its usual state. "No. I don't care. Parties are stupid anyway."

I flashed on all the times in my past when I had missed out on parties and social gatherings and could not understand why. The way I acted when I did not fit in was much different from the way Billy acted. But I knew that underneath his attempts to be tough and cool, he was probably feeling a lot like I used to feel. And that pained look on his face that seemed to come and go for fleeting moments during our conversation convinced me of that even more.

"You know, Billy, acknowledging that you do care is gonna be a really important part of solving your social mystery and changing things for the better. Trust me on that, okay?"

Billy did not answer, but the lack of an answer was much better than another defensive "I don't care," so I took that as a good sign.

"Okay then," I said in a softer and more compassionate voice than I had used with Billy before. "So I'll meet you at the park at four o'clock, okay?"

Billy nodded, and we parted ways.

Can You Solve the Mystery of Billy's Burst Bubble?

Here are some questions that might help you in solving the case:

- How would you describe the mystery?

- What are the facts in this case?

- How would you make sense of the facts?

- What are the biggest clues?

- What does Billy see as the problem?

- What do you think Johnny would see as the problem?

- Why do you think Johnny wants to show Billy the tape?

- What do you think Johnny will say about the tape?

- Why do you think Billy was not invited to the party?

- Why do you think Billy said the kids where jealous of him?

- Do you think you would be friends with Billy? Why?

- What social remedies would you offer to Billy?

- How would you test out your social remedies to see if they were working?

Cracking
the Case

Friday, 3:58 PM

I approached the park bench where Billy was sitting. As I got closer, I realized that he hadn't seen me yet. He was staring down and picking at the hole in the knee of his jeans. I watched him and let my senses take in what his body language was communicating.

What was really interesting about Billy was that his body language always seemed to communicate something completely different when he did not realize anyone was looking at him.

I approached as slowly and quietly as possible so I could see the real Billy. Billy was one of those kids who always seemed to be trying to act a certain way when he was with other people. He was always wearing his social mask. Our "social mask" is the way we act in front of other people to try to convince them we are something we are not. The truth is we all wear social masks sometimes. But ideally, we don't wear our mask too much. It's better to let other people see who we really are.

The most tragic part was that Billy's social mask did not help him socially. Instead, it actually hurt him. His social mask was rude and obnoxious, and pushed people away.

I approached Billy undetected, and what I saw at that moment was not the nasty bully he presented to the world. What I saw was a sad, lonely, insecure kid. I wanted to remember the feeling I was getting from Billy when he was off guard. I wanted to remember because this maskless boy was so much easier to have empathy for.

I knew that as soon as he spotted me, this softer, much more human boy would once again disappear behind the mask. Sure enough, the moment Billy spotted me, his softness and sadness disappeared behind the wannabe cool mask of Billy Bullington.

"What took you, Multony? You know I'm paying you for this," he said as he straightened his body and slipped his "I wanna be cool" bully mask on.

I ignored his banter. "Remember the boy behind the mask," I told myself before saying, "I want to show you something, Billy, and I want you to look very closely."

I pulled out my video camera and sat down beside him on the bench. The little monitor screen lit up with the image of Billy slumped over and deep in thought, without his usual social mask. Then, as he gazed ahead, you could see him light up, his body posture straightening and his face getting an almost excited look. He moved towards Stan and started hassling him.

As Billy watched Stan flailing about in response to his harassment, he began to laugh. I paused the tape.

"So that's funny to you, huh?"

"Well, yeah. I mean look at him all upset. It's pretty funny."

I turned Billy's attention to the other kids on the video. "Look at the other kids around you and Stan," I said. "Tell me what you see."

"All the other kids are watching how I'm playing around with Stan. They are enjoying the show," he said, as he chuckled to himself.

"It's true they are all watching the commotion, but look a little closer, Billy. Look at their facial expressions."

You would have to be blind not to notice the synchronized eye rolling, head shaking and looks of disgust that came from the kids who witnessed Billy's obnoxious behavior. Billy was quiet as he looked at the screen.

"Do they seem entertained to you, Billy?" I asked. "Or do they seem kind of disgusted?"

Billy didn't say anything, but his face was looking more and more serious. I actually thought he might be getting it. "This might be easier than I expected," I thought to myself.

But just then the tape came to the part where Billy grabbed Stan's banana, and Stan started waving his arms wildly.

The Case of Billy's Burst Bubble

Laughter erupted from the kids around them, and I'm embarrassed to say you could hear me, the cameraman who was documenting all this, laughing as well.

"See, Johnny, they think it's funny," he said. "You had me worried for a minute there. But the other kids get it, and they think it's funny."

"Keep watching, Billy, and listen closely."

I turned up the volume on the video recorder so we could better hear everything. The kids on the tape started moving towards the cafeteria. It was hard to make out who was who in all the commotion, but it was easy to hear what the kids were saying as they passed by.

"Billy is such a jerk." "What an idiot." "How can he treat Stan like that? Stan's a cool guy." "Billy is such a loser."

Billy's eyes were fixed on the video screen. The message was painfully clear – the kids thought he was a jerk.

Billy seemed stunned. "You made that last part up right, Johnny? You just added those voices to try and teach me a lesson or something, right?"

"No. That's all real, Billy," I answered.

"I don't believe it. I mean, no one ever says that to me."

"People are scared of you, Billy. But don't mix up being scared with respect. And I'll tell you, that's the way people talk about you all the time," I said with a very serious tone in my voice.

At that point I think I heard the sound of Billy's social mask falling from his face and shattering on the ground into a million pieces.

Billy looked like he was about to cry, and then he ran away from me, towards the grove of trees on the other side of the park. I saw him slow down and sit at the foot of a tall oak tree. Sometimes people need a little space when they are feeling really bad. And in a situation like this, feeling bad can be a good thing. Billy needed to see how others saw him and feel how that felt. Sometimes that is the only thing that can motivate someone to change his or her behavior.

After a few minutes, I walked over to Billy and sat down next to him. "That's hard to hear, huh?" I said in a soft voice.

"Is that really how people see me, Johnny?"

"I'm afraid so, Billy. I'm afraid so."

"So do you think that's why I didn't get invited to Samantha's party?"

"I'm sure of it, Billy."

The Case of Billy's Burst Bubble

"I'm gonna tell you something, Johnny, but you gotta promise not to tell anyone."

"Detective's honor," I said.

"The reason I hassle people, its 'cauz I want to be that cool, tough kid. It's my way of trying to be cool, and I thought kids kind of respected me for that. But that tape just messes with my reality," he said with a little quiver in his voice.

"Even though it can be painful, it's good to see the truth, Billy. And you know what? It's really good to see the real you." I explained the idea of the social masks to Billy and told him how much more likable he was when he was not wearing his bully mask.

"Well, if kids were nicer to me and paid more attention to me, then I wouldn't have to bully them around to get their attention and respect," Billy commented.

"That type of thinking is at the root of your problem, Billy," I explained. "The only way you are going to change your situation is to start taking responsibility for your actions. You have a lot of power over how people act towards you, but when you put all the responsibility on them, you give away your power. You can't change other people. You can only change yourself. And there are a lot of things you can do, if you take responsibility for you actions. There are a lot of things you can do to help get people to respond to you in a more positive way."

Billy picked at the grass and didn't say anything. I could tell the idea of taking responsibility was not something he was familiar with, so I let him sit with it for a while. The patch of grass in front of him got thinner and thinner as he picked at it. Finally, Billy looked up from the now sizable bald patch.

He let out a sigh and asked, "So what do you think I need to change?"

"Well, to start off, I think it would help a lot if you could get a sense of how others might feel when you harass them. You seem to be unaware of how others are reacting to you. Like when you saw the video just now, I don't think you were really tuned in to Stan's or the other kids' reactions. So let's take another look."

I replayed the part of the tape where Billy was bullying Stan and looked up expectantly at Billy.

"So, how do you think Stan was feeling?"

"Well, at the time I was kinda thinking about how I could be funny, but looking at the tape now, I guess he didn't seem to be feeling too good about it."

"That's a good start, Billy. I think that part of your problem is that you are usually too busy thinking about how you can be cool rather than thinking about how you are making other people feel. But the truth is that people are going to see you as much cooler and likable if you are paying attention and responding to how they are feeling."

"I'm not sure I can do that 'paying attention to other people's feelings' thing. That's not how I roll, ya know what I mean? Even if I wanted to, I'm not sure I'd be able to do that," Billy added.

"It is something that takes practice. But you are capable of understanding how others are feeling, Billy. If you weren't, you wouldn't have known that Stan was upset when you looked at the video just now. But most of the time you're probably not thinking about those kinds of things. I'd suggest you make a serious effort to observe others more. Notice their body language and facial expressions. Notice the tone of their voice and what they are saying.

"I'd also suggest trying to ask people questions about themselves. Not only will this help you be more aware of other people's feelings, it will also help you to have more positive interactions with people. When you ask people questions about themselves, you are demonstrating that you are interested in them and not just in yourself. People like it when others are interested in them. It makes them feel good and increases the likelihood that they will feel more positive about you and want to spend more time around you."

Billy was looking at me, but the expression on his face seemed kind of ... well, it was the slightly smirking, slightly dim look that he often wore. But at least he was looking, so I made the call that he was with me, and I continued …

"Another thing I think would really help you is to try being more cooperative with people and less competitive. You brag a lot, Billy. And you always put people down. Those things create a lot of negativity in a relationship and reinforce people's opinion of you as an obnoxious guy who they don't want to be around."

"But that's just the way I am, Johnny. I'm not sure how else I could relate to people."

"Well, in addition to asking people questions about themselves, you could try to compliment others once in a while. When you offer compliments and point out good things about others, you are being cooperative rather than competitive. I guarantee people will respond much better to that than they do to your put-downs and bragging."

"So you think that will make people think I'm cool?" Billy asked.

"I'd suggest that at first you think in terms of people not seeing you as a jerk. Then you can worry about being cool. But the truth is that kids are probably not going to respond to you right away. Everyone is used to you being pretty rude, and at first they will probably take your being nice as some sort of trick. But be persistent and keep trying to be positive. It will eventually pay off.

The Case of Billy's Burst Bubble

"One of most effective things you can do to help change kids' negative view of you is to take responsibility for the way you've been acting. You need to make amends to the kids you've been obnoxious to."

"Make amends?" Billy repeated with a slightly confused look on his face.

"'Amends' means to make up for something you did wrong," I explained. "The best way to start making amends is to let people know you realize you treated them bad and that you're sorry for what you did.

"Tell them how you think they may have felt when you bullied them. If you're really feeling brave, you might even want to tell them why you did it."

"I'm not going to do that. That's just too much," Billy said.

"You don't have to tell them everything, but you might want to tell them how you were just trying to be funny and didn't realize at the time that it was hurtful."

"I'll think about that," Billy said. He lowered his gaze to the ground in front of him and picked a few more blades of grass. "There's a lot I need to think about," he added in a soft voice.

He looked up at me, and I looked back and gave a little smile. His face looked different. It was softer and more thoughtful. It was nice to see the boy behind the bully mask.

"Hey, Johnny," Billy said in a friendly tone.

"Yeah?"

"Sorry for having an attitude with you today. Uh, well, sometimes, I … you know … sometimes I say things to try and be funny and don't realize how it might actually be irritating."

"Thanks for that, Billy. You are so much more likeable when you're not wearing that bully mask."

"Really?" Billy asked.

"Really," I said, feeling for the first time that there might actually be hope for Billy Bullington. "Just remember," I said. "You catch more flies with honey than you do with vinegar. Being sweet will always get you more friends than being … vinegary."

 Billy laughed. "Pickles have a lot of vinegar," he said. "And I like pickles."

"Yeah, but you probably wouldn't ask a pickle over to your house to play after school, would ya? So I think that if you just remember not to be a pickle you'll be okay.

"This mystery is solved!" I said. And for the first time in my knowing Billy Bullington, I gave him a high five.

Chapter 6

It's Not What You Say But How You Say It: The Case of the Back-Talking Ballerina

his semester I had the incredibly good fortune of being elected class messenger. I know class messenger doesn't have the same glamour and prestige that being class president does. It doesn't have the same classy ring as class treasurer. But from my point of view, it is the best job in all of student government.

The class president has to go to those meetings after school every single Thursday. The class treasurer has to keep track of the money and help arrange all the fundraising events like bake sales, and personally I'm not real big on baking.

But the messenger's sole responsibility is to relay information between the teacher and the office. Let me put that another way. The messenger's job is to get up in the middle of class and leisurely walk the halls in the general direction of the office with a special hall pass that grants free passage on campus at a time when you really should be in class.

Then you pick up or drop off whatever information you're supposed to "messenger" and repeat the heavenly, unrushed journey back to class. For me, whenever I'm called to duty, the words that go through my head are "bonus recess." Messenger is without a doubt the best job in all of student government.

Today my very important messenger duty was to turn in the signed field trip permission slips to the office. We are going to the science museum tomorrow. I love science, so for me the whole field trip will be like a bonus recess.

As I strolled down the hall imagining how the science museum would break up the monotony of the daily school routine, my daydreaming was abruptly interrupted by the sound of Mrs. Mannerly's classroom door being thrown open and banging against the wall behind it.

The bang was followed by a series of huffs and puffs coming out of the mouth of one Sassy Underwood. Sassy is tall and thin with short, jet-black hair. She has the body of a dancer, which makes sense given the fact that she is a dancer, and from what I've heard a really good one.

Sassy was featured on the poster for the upcoming dance concert. It was a picture of her in her leotard, gracefully flying through the air doing some type of pirouette dance move thingy. I don't know the exact name for the move, but it looked really cool.

Sassy stormed out of class with so much intensity that I seriously thought I could make out little tiny sparks shooting off her.

"What's up, Sassy?" I asked.

Sassy was so absorbed in her inner turmoil that she hadn't noticed me and jumped a little when I spoke.

"You should watch it, Johnny! You almost gave me a heart attack!" she said in what seemed like an irritated voice.

But I wasn't sure if the irritation was directed at me or was left over from whatever it was that had made her huff and puff out of class.

I asked her again what was up, and followed those words with "Is everything okay?"

"Everything is not okay, Johnny. I was kicked out of class … again! This is the third time this week. I swear my teachers must have it out for me."

I noticed that clenched in Sassy's fist was a slightly crumpled pink piece of paper. Everyone in school knew what a pink slip meant. Like my messenger hall pass, it was a ticket to the office. But while my nicely laminated, multicolored pass bestowed upon the person who carried it a sort of honor, the pink slip gave the clear message to all who saw it that the holder of the slip was in some sort of trouble.

"Off to the office, Sassy?" I said in a gentle voice. "I'm going there, too."

"Yeah, but it's not the same, now is it, Johnny?" Sassy said, again in that irritated tone.

"So what exactly did you do to get kicked out of class, Sassy?"

"I told you, Johnny, my teacher is out to get me. Mrs. Mannerly called on me to solve a math problem on the board, and I went up and answered it. I got the answer right. Then she handed me this pink slip and told me to go to the office."

Sassy held up the pink slip and tightened her fist around it.

"Come on," I said. "There has got to be more to the story than that. I know Mrs. Mannerly can be strict, but even she wouldn't send you to the office for no reason."

"Hello, Johnny. What part of 'the teacher is out to get me' don't you understand? Aren't you supposed to be one of those brainy-type kids?"

Had I not been so intrigued by the idea of Mrs. Mannerly sending Sassy out of the classroom for no reason, I probably would have been irritated by the tone Sassy was taking with me. But at that moment I was more focused on the mystery. There had to be some reason why Mrs. Mannerly had sent Sassy out. Why didn't Sassy know the reason? Why would she just think the teachers were out to get her?

Sassy and I walked silently towards the office, both absorbed in our own thoughts. As we approached our destination, Sassy finally broke the silence.

"You know, Johnny, if I keep getting in trouble …" Her voice trailed off, and she stared down at her feet as she walked. "If I keep getting in trouble like this, something bad is gonna happen."

Sassy's voice was much calmer, and she seemed less defensive. Her tone of voice and her body language made me think she might be more open to looking at what might really be going on.

"What do you think is going to happen?" I asked.

"Well, one thing is for sure. If I keep getting in trouble, I won't be able to perform in the dance concert next week. I couldn't handle that, Johnny. Dancing is my life. But I just keep getting these nasty little pink slips."

She held up the slip and looked at it for a second, then let her arm drop down and her gaze fall back to the floor in front of her.

"Maybe it would help to see if there's some reason the teachers seem out to get you," I suggested.

"I can't imagine why they would be like that, Johnny. I try to be a good student. I participate in class. I do all my work. I get good grades."

"It's a social mystery then," I said, trying to hide the excitement in my voice. Just the idea of a social mystery always gets me excited. But Sassy's tone was not at all excited, and if I were to show excitement in response to her trouble, it would probably offend her and make her feel like I did not get how she was feeling.

People feel understood when we respond to them with a tone or mood that matches their own. And often people feel misunderstood, or like we don't care, when the tone of our response does not match their mood.

"So what ... you want me to pay you to help me? Is that it, Mr. Social Detective?" Sassy said in a voice that sounded like she was accusing me of doing something terrible.

"You can do whatever you want. I'm just saying it sounds like a mystery to me." I was extra careful not to react to Sassy's irritation. While it is often helpful to match people's feelings and moods, if you match someone's irritation, it's likely to make things worse rather than better.

"Well, if I were to hire you, Johnny, what would you do, and how much do you charge?" Sassy asked after another long pause.

The Case of the Back-Talking Ballerina

"It's a dollar a day plus expenses. And what I would do is help you get to the bottom of all this and figure out just what is going on."

We had arrived at the office by now. I went up to the counter to turn in the permission slips, and Sassy sat down on *the bench*.

The bench is where kids who get in trouble and are sent to the office sit while they await their sentencing. I couldn't even begin to imagine how many kids had sat there awaiting their doom over the years. While I've been fortunate never to have been sent to *the bench* for sentencing, I did sit there once while I waited for a package to bring back to class. When I sat there, I swear I could feel the dread of all the kids who had perched on that seat over the years, waiting for the principal to come and lead them into his chamber of doom for sentencing. Just thinking about it gave me a major case of the heebeegeebees.

"I have some papers for you to bring back to class, Johnny. Just have a seat, and I'll give them to you in a minute," Mrs. Orderly, the office manager, told me, pointing towards *the bench*.

"I'll just stand, Mrs. Orderly. Thanks," I said as a slight chill went up my spine at the thought of having to sit there again.

I turned and brought my attention back to Sassy. Her body was slumped, chin resting in her hand, supporting the weight of her head. Her face was the face of someone who had a lot of heavy thoughts going on inside, so it was no wonder she needed to hold her head up.

I don't know if it was my personal feelings about *the bench* or the heavy look on Sassy's face, but all I could think in looking at Sassy was "dread." How I wanted to grab her hand and flee the office before the principal's door opened and Sassy was led to her doom. Sassy could run and never come back. She could go to another school, another town, flee across the border to Mexico like they do in the movies and start a whole new life. Okay, probably not my best idea.

"I'm afraid that if things don't change, something really bad is going to happen, Johnny." Sassy pulled out a dollar bill and handed it to me. "So what should I do?" she asked.

"Just go about your day, Sassy, and I'll get to work on your case," I reassured

As I left the office and headed back to class, I started planning how to collect the facts I needed to solve this case. Solving the case was a much better plan than fleeing to Mexico, but it was going to be tricky because I didn't have any classes with Sassy, and her mystery involved her relationship with her teachers. Fortunately, we had the school field trip the next day, and our classes were going together.

Thursday, 8:32 AM

You could hear the hum of the bus motors outside as the students who were lucky enough to be missing class and going on the field trip migrated towards the front of the school.

The Case of the Back-Talking Ballerina

The sound of the motors mixed with the buzz of excitement that was building among the kids, making it difficult to hear the teachers giving directions. Usually on field trips I position myself strategically in the bus line so I can be next to my friends. But today I was on a case, so my priorities had changed.

Normally, this kind of surveillance would call for my spy listening device; however, the teachers had given specific instructions that absolutely no Game Boys, iPods or anything like that were allowed on the trip. So if I was spotted with an electronic device, it could not only blow my cover, it could also get me in serious trouble. I had to find a way to stay close enough to Sassy that I could hear without the aid of my nifty surveillance tool.

I entered the bus line about ten kids behind Sassy. We filed onto the bus, and I took a seat three rows back and on the opposite side from Sassy. This was the perfect spot for surveillance. Next to me sat Shae Nanagens. This was a potential problem because Shae had a tendency to be a class clown, and I didn't want him to draw any unwarranted attention. Good surveillance involves a certain quality of invisibility, and class clowns like Shae always seemed to do everything in their power to be visible.

I opened my detective notebook and began to gather the facts. Sassy was sitting next to her friend Anya. Anya is a really cool, smart, creative kid who everyone seems to like. Anya and Sassy chatted away while the teachers did their head count, making sure all the kids who were supposed to be on the bus were there.

"I need everyone to stop talking and listen up," Arthur Ity, the gym teacher, announced in a strong, booming voice.

At just that moment, Sassy and Anya giggled about something they had been discussing. Mr. Ity looked at them with eyes that said in no uncertain terms, "You two are on the verge of very big trouble."

Now Arthur Ity's eyes always seem to say that even when he is laughing and joking around. But it still was intimidating. Anya gave Mr. Ity a sweet smile and looked down at her hands. Sassy, on the other hand, looked at Mr. Ity, rolled her eyes and then stared off in air. Mr. Ity zeroed in on Sassy, moving his face close to hers.

"Did you hear what I said, Miss Underwood?"

"Yeah, yeah, I heard you," Sassy replied.

"Well, just to make sure, I'm gonna have you come sit up front with me."

Sassy's seat change was unexpected and put a major snag in my fact gathering. But it was just as well, because five minutes into the bus ride, Shea Nanaggins announced to me and everyone else within ear shot that he was bored. And when someone like Shae starts to get bored, you know the clowning is about to begin.

I counted seven attempts by teachers to get Shae back in his seat, lower his voice, not touch someone, and my personal favorite, "JUST STOP, SHAE!"

"Just stop, Shae" was one of the most frequent statements to come out of teachers' mouths in class. Sometimes it was hard to pinpoint exactly what they wanted Shae to stop doing. But we all knew what it meant, because often Shae was a sort of indefinable flurry of activity, and by the time you said stop, he had usually already stopped whatever he had been doing and moved on to something else that was equally annoying.

So, "Just stop Shae" seemed to refer to a more general state of commotion than any one specific event. It was very interesting, even though a sense of commotion always seemed to follow Shea around, he still had pretty good relationships with the teachers. And, considering how often they had to reel him in, he did not seem to get in that much trouble.

We arrived at the science center around 9:45 AM and lined up outside the entrance, in as orderly a fashion as a busload of kids on a field trip are capable. Sassy quickly reunited with Anya as well as with a few other girls she was friends with. I positioned myself behind their pack and brought my attention back to my detective work.

Mr. Ity's voice cut through the buzz of chatter. It kind of felt like a small earthquake in your body when he spoke, and everyone got quiet. "Okay everyone, listen up. We have six wonderful guides to tour us through the science center. That means I need six groups. So start grouping up. Ten to 15 kids per group. If you can't group up quickly and orderly on your own, I'll have to group you myself." Mr. Ity then motioned to the tour guides and moved his hands like a traffic cop directing cars at a busy intersection.

The kids started to form their packs. Ten to 15 kids was the perfect number for detective work. Not too small to be conspicuous and not so big that there would be lots of people to interfere with my fact gathering. I blended into the group that Sassy and her friends had joined.

My buddies JD and Dave motioned me to come hang with them in another group, but I was on a case. I smiled, pointed to the group I was in, waved my detective notebook inconspicuously and shrugged my shoulders. They both threw their hands up, smiled and waved. Fortunately, I have good friends who understand that sometimes the work of a social detective means having to sacrifice quality time with your bros. That's part of the price you pay for being a social detective.

"Hello, everyone. My name is Maria, and I will be taking you around the science center today," our young, bubbly guide announced in a musical, upbeat tone.

The Case of the Back-Talking Ballerina

She began by telling us about all the ways science had changed our lives and all the technology we use every day that is a result of the hard work of scientists.

"Did you know that if it wasn't for scientists, we would still be using candles to see at night? Without scientists, there would be no light bulbs and no electricity to light up the light bulbs."

"You don't have to be a rocket scientist to figure that one out," Sassy said in a tone that seemed a little irritated.

Our guide chuckled uncomfortably at Sassy's comment but went on. "Can anyone tell me who invented the light bulb?" Maria asked in a perky voice.

"Everyone knows that," Sassy blurted out in that same, slightly irritated-sounding voice. "It's Thomas Edison."

"Yes, that's right. But please, let's raise our hands, okay?" Maria said trying to keep her upbeat attitude.

I could tell by the look on Maria's face and from the slight change in the music of her voice that Sassy's style of communicating was bothering her.

"Whatever. I was just trying to participate," Sassy said in a voice that was dripping with attitude.

"Uh, okay, well uh, Thomas Edison is a great example of someone who used science to help create innovations that affect how we live our lives every day."

You could tell our guide was a little flustered by Sassy's attitude, but she moved on with her presentation. Maria talked about electricity as we walked. She led us to a big open area with some interesting-looking gadgets and then stopped.

"Can anyone tell me who discovered electricity?" she asked the group.

"Oh, oh, it was Benjamin Franklin, right?" Kenneth blurted out enthusiastically.

"Ahh. That's a really good guess," Maria said. "Benjamin Franklin did study electricity and had some interesting theories about it, but most people agree that it was William Gilbert in the late 1500s who first really studied electricity. And it was the German physicist Otto von Guericke who created the first electrical generator in 1663. It produced static electricity. And I know all of you have experienced that before. It's that little shock you get when you touch something after rubbing your feet on the carpet, for example."

"Otto von Guericke. Am I really supposed to care about that?" Sassy mumbled in a not-so quiet voice to Anya. Anya ignored her and kept her attention on the guide. It also seemed like Anya took a little step away from Sassy after she said that.

The Case of the Back-Talking Ballerina

"Now I need some volunteers to come up and help me," announced Maria. Responses to the call for volunteers always tell you something about people. There are the people who like to participate and the people who like to watch. And whenever the call for volunteers happens, those who like to participate shoot their hands up and do the little "pick me, pick me" dance, while those who like to watch get really still and seem to shrink a little, as if they are trying to turn themselves invisible so no one will call on them.

Sassy was a participator, and she waved her arms to try to get Maria's attention. Maria picked Anya and Kenneth and then, after a long pause, seemingly hesitantly, she picked Sassy.

"Static electricity can give you a shock, but it also does something else that is very interesting." Maria pulled out a long pole and waved it in the air. "No, it's not a light saber. It's an electricity rod. But sometimes I call it my hair saber."

Maria motioned to Anya to come forward. Anya's eyes got big, and she made a comical, pretend scared face. Anya has beautiful long red hair, and when Maria held the rod over Anya's head and pressed the button, almost all of Anya's silky mane shot straight up towards the electric hair saber.

Anya's eyes got even bigger, and she started to laugh. The rest of us joined in. It was a funny sight. "Static electricity loves hair," Maria said in her perky voice. Then she let go of the button, and Anya's hair drifted back down.

"Thank you, Anya," Maria said. "Now let's see what electricity can do to this light bulb."

Maria now pulled out a light bulb the size of a bowling ball and handed it to Kenneth. Then she took a long cord with sockets on the ends and handed one end to Sassy. She explained the route of electricity from the electric plant through the wires in your home to the bulb.

"What I want you to do is touch the end of the light bulb to the socket Sassy is holding, and then I'm going to touch the electricity rod to the other socket, and let's see what happens, alright?"

Sassy cocked her head to the side and scrunched her face up in just the way to give the classic example of a kid with a really bad attitude. Even though we were not supposed to have any electronics on the trip, I had smuggled my cell phone onto the bus. At this point, I carefully snuck it out of my pocket and snapped a picture of Sassy. It was just too perfect a clue to pass up.

"This better not make my hair stand up, and I better not get a shock," Sassy announced.

Maria did not respond to Sassy as she touched the rod to the socket. "This is how much energy I used to make Anya's hair stand up," Maria announced.

The Case of the Back-Talking Ballerina

There was a faint glow in the light bulb. "And this is how much you need to really light up that big bulb."

As she cranked up the power, the rod made a buzzing sound, and the bulb erupted with bright white light. The combination of the buzzing sound and the flash of light was like fireworks, and everyone ooohed and awed. Everyone, that is, except Sassy! Sassy's face looked bored and slightly irritated. It even looked to me like see was rolling her eyes.

After a very cool and interesting tour, we headed for the grand finale of our science center adventure. It was a screening of a 3-D IMAX movie about strange, gigantic fish that lived deep in the sea.

The movie screen was literally the size of a building. Looking up at it as you entered the theater made you dizzy. We all filed into the rows of seats in the humongous room; I positioned myself in the row just behind Sassy and her friends.

"Watch it," Sassy blurted out to her friend Debbie, who seemed to bump into her accidentally as they moved down the narrow row of seats.

"It was an accident, Sassy, chill out," Debbie said in a slightly irritated voice.

I have to admit that once the lights went out and the movie started, I completely lost track of Sassy and her mystery. All

I could think about at that point was the strange giant three-dimensional fish popping out at me from the biggest movie screen I had ever seen. It was amazing. And it was okay that I lost my focus at that point. I had all the facts I needed.

After the movie we all had lunch in the science center cafeteria. I noticed Sassy sitting alone. I wrote a few final notes down in my detective notebook and then looked around to find Dave and JD. This case was solved, and it was time to hang out with my buddies.

 Can You Solve the Case of the Back-Talking Ballerina?

Here are some questions that might help you in solving the case:

- How would you describe the mystery?

- What are the facts in this case?

- How would you make sense of the facts?

- What are the biggest clues?

- What does Sassy see as the problem?

- What do you think Johnny would see as the problem?

- What clues did Johnny find to help him solve the case?

- Was Sassy treated more harshly by teachers than other kids, and if so, why?

- Why did Mr. Ity move Sassy's seat and not Anya's?

- Do you think you would be friends with Sassy? Why?

- What social remedies would you offer to Sassy?

- How would you test out your social remedies to see if they were working?

 Cracking the Case

I sat with my friends on the bus on the way back to school. There was no need to gather any more facts. The solution to Sassy's social mystery had pretty much wrapped itself up with a pretty little bow and plopped itself down right in front of me.

We arrived back at school just before the dismissal bell rang. I caught up with Sassy and asked her to join me on the playground so we could talk. We sat down by the big tree, and I proceeded to let her know I had solved her mystery.

"Yeah, well, spit it out," she said, in what I was starting to recognize as her normal feisty way of communicating with people.

"Have you ever heard the word 'feisty' before?" I started.

Sassy laughed. "Only every day from my parents," she said with a smirk on her face. "They seem to think I'm feisty."

"Well, do you see that in yourself?"

"Parents always call their kids feisty, Johnny. Come on, you should know that."

"Well, feisty can mean a lot of different things, Sassy. It can mean lively and full of energy. Or it can mean someone who is hostile and combative when interacting with others."

"I'm not a hostile person, Johnny. I only get hostile when I'm not being treated fairly. Like when teachers are out to get me. Did you see what Mr. Ity did on the bus today when Anya and I were talking? Now I know we shouldn't have been talking, but he totally had it out for me. He made me go sit in front with him and didn't say anything to Anya."

"I know, Sassy. I saw. Do you have any idea why you were singled out?"

Sassy looked at me with an expression that very effectively communicated to me, "Are you an idiot, Johnny?"

"Uhhhh, because the teachers are out to get me? Isn't that what I've been saying the whole time?" she said in a voice that fit perfectly with her facial expression.

The Case of the Back-Talking Ballerina

"Okay, Sassy. This isn't gonna work unless you start to look for explanations for things other than your claim that people are out to get you. So let's start by assuming that there is some reason why people are reacting to you the way they are.

"And why don't we start right here and now? Do you realize how you just spoke to me? Do you realize what your face looked like and how your voice sounded?"

"What's wrong with my face?" Sassy asked.

"Here, I'll show you," I said.

I opened my eyes wide, dropped one eyebrow and raised the other, lifted the right side of my mouth, and tilted and shook my head disapprovingly, with the best "Are you an idiot?" facial impression I could do.

"I don't look like that, Johnny."

"I'm afraid you do, Sassy."

I pulled out my mobile phone and showed her the picture I had taken when she was holding the electric cord during the demonstration earlier in the day.

She stared silently. "That's not that bad. I … I mean, that picture looks worse than it is. I wasn't really feeling that … You know. I wasn't feeling as bad as that picture looks. I'm sure people would know I was just exaggerating."

"I didn't know that, Sassy. And I'm a social detective. How would other people know it?"

Sassy looked at me, and I could tell she was thinking.

"Okay. Let me ask you this, Sassy. What would you think if you were to see someone making that face?"

She looked back at the picture and then up at me, then back at the picture again.

"I guess I'd think they were pretty obnoxious," she said in a softer voice than the one she had been using up to that point.

"Yup. That would be the perfect word to describe it," I agreed.

"But things build up. I mean Mr. Ity, the way he treated me made me so frustrated. It wasn't fair."

"But there is a reason why he treated you that way, Sassy. You have a lot more power over how people react to you than I think you realize. Do you know why Mr. Ity sent you to the front of the bus and not Anya?" I asked.

"Yeah, because he hates me!"

"No, I don't think that's it. I think it's because of how you responded to him when he asked you to stop talking. Do you remember how you responded to him?"

The Case of the Back-Talking Ballerina

"Anya and I were just joking around, but I stopped talking right after he said something," Sassy explained with a defensive tone in her voice.

"When Mr. Ity stared at you and Anya, you stared off into space and rolled your eyes. What message do you think that communicated to him?" I asked.

"I don't know. I wasn't thinking about it at the time. I was just irritated."

"Your response communicated that you were irritated, Sassy. And by looking off into space and rolling your eyes, you also gave the message that you were not paying attention to Mr. Ity or respecting his authority. Anya, on the other hand, looked Mr. Ity in the eyes, then smiled and looked down, which communicated a sense of respect for him.

"Facial expressions and body language communicate a lot. But to add to that, when Mr. Ity asked you if you'd heard him, you said, 'Yeah, yeah, I heard you,' in a voice that also communicated a lack of respect for his authority. And do you know what teachers almost always do when you don't show them that you have respect for their authority? They demonstrate how they really do have authority over you. And that's exactly what Mr. Ity did with you. He didn't do that with Anya because she was respectful from the beginning.

"Speaking of respect," I continued, "do you think you were respectful with our guide Maria from the science center?"

"Okay, now what did I do?" Sassy asked, rolling her eyes again.

"So, how about that response, Sassy? Did you notice your tone of voice and how you rolled your eyes just now?"

"I can't help it, Johnny. I'm just irritated. Don't you ever get irritated?"

"Sure, Sassy. I definitely get irritated. Like when people talk to me in an irritated voice and roll their eyes when I'm trying to help them," I said with a big smile and a slightly silly look on my face that was meant to convey the message that I was not taking what I was saying too seriously and that I was not really that irritated with her.

"I'm sorry, Johnny. Sometimes I get really irritated, and I don't think about those kind of things."

"I can understand that, Sassy. I have some suggestions for how to address that, which we can talk about in a little while. But first let's get clearer on what's going on that makes other people respond to you the way they do. When you can fully understand what you might be doing that leads to people reacting the way they do, you will have more power over how people respond to you.

"With Maria, the guide, you said things and acted in ways that were not very respectful. You said things like, 'You don't have to be a rocket scientist to figure that one out,' and 'Everyone knows that.' Your body language and facial expressions, as well as your tone of voice, also communicated a lot. And the way you communicated directly affected the way Maria responded to you.

"Did you notice that Maria made a comment about you not raising your hand and just blurting out, but did not say that to anyone else who talked without raising their hands?"

"Yeah. Kenneth totally blurted out during the presentation, and Maria didn't say anything to him. Not only did she not say anything, she actually complimented him on his answer, even though his answer was wrong. That just seems so unfair!" Sassy said in a frustrated voice.

"Do you know why Kenneth got a compliment, Sassy? It wasn't for the answer, and it definitely wasn't for blurting out without raising his hand. It was for his enthusiastic attitude. Even though Kenneth did not raise his hand, he had a positive attitude and showed he was interested in what Maria was talking about.

"When people feel you are respectful of them and respond to them in a positive way, they are much more likely not to make a big deal of minor imperfections like talking without raising your hand."

"Is that why Shae gets away with everything?" Sassy asked in a voice that was slightly exasperated but also conveyed a tone of being a little amused.

"It's almost funny sometimes how much Shae seems to get away with, isn't it?" I asked. "And you're right, Sassy. He does get away with more than others, and that's because he has good PR skills."

"What's PR, Johnny?"

"PR stands for 'public relations.' Our public relations refer to how we get along with others. It's about how people see us. And it's about the things we do to affect people's responses to us. While Shae is not so great at following rules and controlling himself, he has very good public relations. Even though he does irritating things, people still seem to like him because he is usually pretty positive and nice to others.

"Even when he is acting sorta crazy, he remains respectful, and the effect is dramatic. Teachers still like him and are much more tolerant of the tornados he creates because his overall relationship with them is good. If it wasn't for his excellent PR, Shae would probably have been kicked out of school a long time ago."

"I guess that makes sense, Johnny."

"We have a lot of power over how others respond to us, Sassy. Our attitude and what we communicate affect what we get back. That's true, not just with teachers and grown-ups, but with friends as well. And I would be careful with your friends, Sassy, because your attitude can have a negative effect on them, too."

The Case of the Back-Talking Ballerina

"I do feel like my friends have been getting more and more irritated with me recently. On the field trip today, Debbie told me to chill out, and then she pretended like she didn't hear me. When I asked her to sit with me on the bus ride home, she went and sat with someone else," Sassy said.

"I hate to say it, Sassy, but it doesn't surprise me."

"Why do you say that, Johnny?"

"When you were in the IMAX movie and Debbie accidentally bumped into you, you got hostile and told her to 'watch it' in a really nasty way. I wish you could have seen the look on your face when you said that. You looked like you were totally disgusted with her."

"I can't help it, Johnny. I seem to get really irritated at times."

"I can understand that you get irritated, Sassy, but do you think that sometimes your irritation is bigger than what the situation calls for?"

Sassy paused, and an irritated look started to come over her face. But then her face softened.

"Maybe. But what can I do when I get so irritated?" she asked.

"That is a great question," I said. "And it is the type of question that can solve problems because it is your actions, not the actions of others, that you have power over.

"I'd say that my first suggestion for you would be to try to be more aware of how others respond to you when you say or do things. That will help you to be more conscious of what you do that works well and what you do that does not work well. When you notice someone responding in a negative way towards you, ask yourself if you had an attitude toward that person. If you did, you can do some damage control right away without giving the negativity time to fester and have even more of a negative impact."

"What do you mean by 'damage control,' Johnny?"

"Damage control is about finding your way back to a positive place with someone after you took things to a negative place. You might do that by acknowledging that what you said, or the way you said it, might have come across as too harsh or negative. Saying 'sorry' is also an excellent form of damage control. Also, if something came out in a negative way, it can be helpful to restate what you said in a way that gets your point across but that is less offensive to the other person.

"For example, had you noticed Debbie's reaction to you when you told her to 'watch it' in a mean voice, you could have said, 'Hey Debbie, I'm sorry. That came out harsher than I meant it. I should have asked in a nicer tone of voice if you could try to be careful because I was getting bumped.'

"Even if you don't do damage control right away, you can still go back and do it later. While you will probably never see

The Case of the Back-Talking Ballerina

Maria again, it's not too late to tell Debbie or Mr. Ity that you are sorry you had an attitude. 'Sorry' can go a long way. It can change the way people see you and make them think about you in a more positive way.

"It would seem completely appropriate to tell your friends and even someone like Mr. Ity that sometimes you have a problem with getting irritated. You can tell them that you're trying not to take it out on them but that, if you do, you hope they don't take it too personally because it's not about them.

"If people know beforehand that your irritation is not necessarily about them, and that you realize that and are working on it, they are less likely to get irritated when you unintentionally snap at them.

"When you snapped at me before, I didn't take it personally because I could tell you were having a problem getting overly irritated and that it was not really about me. But your friends might not realize that and probably need you to spell it out for them.

"Another thing that I think would help with damage control is to build up a reservoir of positive interactions with people. This would give you a cushion to soften the blow if you do get snappy with someone."

"What do you mean by a 'reservoir'?" Sassy asked.

"Well, a reservoir of water is a basically a supply of water. If you have a drought, your reservoir of water will keep you supplied with water until it rains again. In relationships, you can build a reservoir of positive feelings, so if something negative happens, there are some positive feelings stored up to help you get through it.

"If you have a lot of good experiences with a friend and something negative happens, the impact of the negative will be softened by the fresh memories of all the positive interactions and feelings between you and your friend.

"In such a situation, you will probably say something like 'This is negative, but overall we have a lot of good things in our relationship, so it's not that big a deal. I know that we still really like each other.' But if there is not a reservoir of positive interactions and feelings, the negative interaction will probably have a much bigger effect."

"I can see that. I think I've had a reservoir built up with my friends, but it seems to be running low recently because they seem to be getting more and more irritated with me," Sassy said with a slightly pained look on her face.

"It's not too late to build that reservoir back up."

"So how do I build my reservoir back up, Johnny?"

"There are lots of ways you can do that. Try to think of things you do when you are irritated and then do the exact opposite. Instead of saying something mean and critical, you can compliment someone or say something supportive. For example, with Maria, instead of saying, 'Everybody knows that' in response to her question, you could have said, 'That's a great question. I know the answer.'

"You could try to point out the good things people do and tell them things you like about them. It is also important to remember that a big part of what we communicate to people comes from things other than our actual words. Our facial expressions communicate a lot to people. When you feel like giving someone a dirty look, offer a smile instead. The music in our voice also communicates a lot to people."

"Music?" Sassy repeated with a quizzical look on her face.

"Yeah. There is a lot of music in what people say that affects us, even though we might not be aware of it. Most people have a melody to their voice that highlights what they are saying. And the melody gives a lot of information.

"It's kind of like what happens when we see a movie. The soundtrack adds an important layer to the movie and conveys a lot about the feeling and the meaning in the movie. Often, we are not even thinking about the soundtrack. But if the soundtrack wasn't there, we would notice. The movie would seem flat and dull.

"The same is true for the music in our voices. While we might not think about it a lot, if it was not there and people just talked like robots, we would notice. And when the music in people's voices is harsh, it has a big effect on us.

"Even if someone is saying something that is not mean, the music can make it sound mean. Here's an example."

I looked Sassy in the eyes and said with an angry, insincere melody in my voice, "I'm sorry I bumped into you."

"Well, what do you think? Was that a good sorry?" I asked with a mischievous grin on my face.

"No. It was really irritating, and it didn't seem like you meant it," Sassy replied.

"Exactly." "Now how about this ..."

I looked Sassy in the eyes again and, with a sweet, sincere melody in my voice, I said, "I'm sorry I bumped into you."

"I get your point, Johnny. That was much better."

"And the only thing different between the first time I said it and the second time was the music in my voice. The music in our voices is a powerful thing. It affects others dramatically and, if you can realize how powerful an effect it has, you will have a lot more power over the way people react to you."

"Those things all sound good, Johnny. But I still get really irritated, and I'm not sure if I will be able to control the music in my voice or the looks on my face or the things I say when I'm so irritated."

The Case of the Back-Talking Ballerina

"Okay. Let's talk about that a little. First, it's important to remember that just being aware of how you are feeling and acting automatically gives you more control over what you express to others. By thinking about your actions, you will have more ability to pause before you act and to choose how you respond, rather than just responding impulsively.

"But the point you bring up is important. How can you be less irritated? There are a lot of reasons we get irritated. You may need to think about what those reasons are to figure them out. It may help to talk to someone else about those feelings, too.

"But in addition to thinking and talking about where the irritation comes from, there are other things you can do. For starters, you can notice how you experience irritation. We were talking about how music affects the way we feel and react when we watch a movie. Well, the sensations in our bodies and the words and images in our heads affect how we feel and react when different things happen in our lives. They affect us in really big ways that we usually don't even realize.

"So you can try and think about what your body feels like when you are irritated. Are there irritated sensations in your body? Do you have irritated thoughts? Do you have irritated images in your head?"

"Yes!" Sassy blurted out emphatically. "I have all of those, and I have them a lot!"

"Okay. So let's start with the way your body feels when you are irritated. One thing that is helpful when your body feels irritated is to notice exactly where the irritated feeling is inside of you. What part of your body feels irritated? Does the irritated feeling have a certain shape? Does it feel tight or loose, hot or cold? Ask yourself questions to find out more about exactly what the irritations feel like.

"When we don't think about exactly how something feels, the feeling stays vague, and we can't do anything to change it. But when we become more aware of how we feel, we can more effectively do something to change it. So once you get a good sense of the feeling in your body, you can do things to soothe it.

"For example, you can try deep breaths or stretching. You can rub the spot where the irritation is the strongest. You can excuse yourself from the situation and run or do push-ups to let out the irritated energy in a way that does not get you in trouble and does not bother other people. If you are alone and no one can hear you, you can even scream to let the feelings out.

"As for the thoughts in your head, it can be helpful to pay close attention to what those irritated thoughts are saying. For example, you can write them down to get a clearer idea of what they are. You can also ask yourself when you notice yourself starting to get irritated, 'What are my irritated thoughts right now?'

"Once you have a clear sense of your thoughts, you can do things to soothe them. You can challenge the thoughts and tell yourself why they are not true. You can also tell yourself it's not that big of a deal and that you are not going to let it get to you. You might also want to try to let your thoughts go to something more pleasant and enjoyable than the thing that is irritating you.

"Finally, if you are having images that are irritating, you can do some of the same things you do with the thoughts in your head. Often we have images in our head that affect the way we feel, but we don't realize it. You might be stressed about taking a test and have the image of your teacher with a disappointed look on his face handing you back a test with a big red F on it. An image like that is bound to make you more anxious about the test.

"To decrease the power that images can have over you, start by noticing if there are any images that go along with your irritated feelings. Notice exactly what those images are. By becoming more aware of the images in your head, you have the opportunity to challenge any negative images that might come up. You might have images of people doing things to irritate you or people with mean looks on their faces or some other images that are irritating to you. When you notice them, you have the power to change them. You can change the image of the situation in which someone is irritating you into one in which someone is doing something similar that does not irritate you. For example, you can change the images of someone giving you a mean look into the image of someone smiling at you.

"You can also replace any irritating images with relaxing images that are soothing and enjoyable. I often imagine surfing at the beach when I'm feeling irritated, and it usually helps me to relax and feel better.

"But I really think that if you work on building your positive reservoir with people, you will start to feel less irritated. Acting in negative ways often makes us feel more negative. But acting in a positive way can often lead to us feeling much more positive inside. A positive attitude can be contagious."

Sassy had been listening carefully. "It's hard, Johnny," she sighed. "Sometimes you get in the habit of being negative, and it happens without you even realizing it."

"That's so true," I agreed. "One thing you can do to break that habit is to think about what you are going to say before you say it. Do a practice run of what you are going to say first, and think about how you would feel if someone said the same thing to you. Putting yourself in others' shoes can help you to be more sensitive about what you are saying. And it can result in much better public relations. Finally, if you notice that you are feeling irritated, it's probably better not to say anything at all. You can always come back later and say what you want to say."

"That's a lot to think about, Johnny. I do like the idea of feeling less irritated and having more of that positive reservoir type thing with people."

Sassy looked at me and smiled really big. It was an exaggerated smile, but it seemed sincere.

 "Thank you for all your help, Johnny. I really appreciate it. You are a good friend," she said, with a very friendly and appreciative melody in her voice.

"Thanks, Sassy. That was nice to hear."

"And you know what, Johnny? It felt really good to say it."

"Well, Sassy. I think this case is officially cracked. Let me now how everything works outs."

"I will, Johnny. Thanks again."

Chapter 7

Drowning in the Details: The Case of Monologuing Mona

It was getting closer to my "favorite" time of the school year. It was the time of the year that came right before open house. Okay, you might have guessed that the reason why I put "favorite" in quotation marks is that I'm being sarcastic. What I really mean is that this is probably my "least favorite" time of the year. Sometimes a little irony helps to take the sting out of unpleasant things, because a little bit of irony can make things humorous.

Anyway, the reason I always dread this time of the year is that it's when teachers start to make us do all the flashy projects to show to parents at open house. Teachers seem to think that flashy projects prove how hard they have been working us kids during the year.

It's not that I mind working hard. In fact, I love giving my mind a good workout and getting my brain all pumped up. I have always thought of doing schoolwork as being like lifting weights. All the work you ever do in school, even if it seems pointless at the time, gives your brain a workout and makes it stronger and more muscular. I love having a buff brain.

But these open house projects are not just about getting a mental workout. They are about creating flashy eye-catchers that all the parents would ooh and aah about. And, of course, flashy eye-catchers always seem to mean the same thing – art projects.

In that time leading up to open house, all the teachers seem to change their prime directive from, let's say, learning science, English, history or important things like that, to creating art projects to impress the parents. Even in math class, Mrs. Krabington was making us create a mobile out of three-dimensional geometric shapes. And we had to color all the shapes, too! I mean, come on. What on earth does coloring have to do with math?

Now, loads of kids love this time of the year. They'd much rather make mobiles out of colorful paper shapes than doing things like math work. But I have never been good at art, so my mobiles always end up looking like something my dog uses as a chew toy. Even though I do great in all my classes, my open house, artsy-type projects end up in the least conspicuous places in the classroom so they would not scare the parents too much.

The Case of Monologuing Mona

Today Mrs. Yano informed us of her plan for the open house razzle dazzle. She is making us do a report on the Civil War that has to include a full three-dimensional diorama showing a scene from the Civil War. Fortunately for me, this will be a group project, and that means there is a chance I can get out of doing the artsy part.

Mrs. Yano announced that it was time to pick partners. Everyone scurried around the class to find kids they wanted to work with. I strategically targeted the kids I thought of as the most artistically inclined. That way I could do the writing part of the report, and they could focus more on the art.

I ended up with Kaia and Thomas in my group. Kaia is a great artist and really smart. Thomas, well, he is a good friend of mine, which obviously counts for a lot. But he is also pretty easygoing and smart.

There was a buzz of chatter as all the students took advantage of the partner-picking time to socialize with their friends.

"All right, everyone. Let's get back to our seats," Mrs. Yano said in an upbeat voice. "Now, is there anyone who does not have a group?"

At first, there was no response. Then, in the front of the room, I saw a lone hand start to rise, then hesitate, then fully rise into the air. It was the hand of one Mona Logging.

I was surprised to see Mona's hand up. She is one of the smartest kids in the class. She is always answering questions and demonstrating in class how much she knows about the things we are talking about. She is the type of kid that everyone usually wants in their group for class projects because you know she will offer a lot to the project. Typically, it is kids like Dimsly Overhead and Billy Bullington who are left out of groups. Not kids like Mona.

"Does anyone have room for another group member?" Mrs. Yano asked, her eyes searching the room for an answer.

No one responded. I couldn't understand it. I didn't have that much contact with Mona, but nothing stood out that would warrant her being shunned by the other kids. This seemed mysterious to me.

But the excitement I usually get from a good social mystery was overshadowed by the sadness I felt for Mona that no one wanted her in their group. I couldn't bear to see Mona shut out like that.

I had felt shut out a lot in the past and knew the feeling well. And because I knew the feeling in a very personal way, I did not want anyone else to have to feel like that. So I raised my hand to signal that Mona could join our group.

I realized that I was making what you call a "unilateral decision." A "unilateral decision" is one that one person makes without consulting others who are affected by the decision. So basically, I was deciding all on my own to invite Mona into our group without consulting with the other group members. It is bad etiquette for friends to make unilateral decisions like that. But I was kinda swept away by the moment.

I looked at Kaia and Thomas as I held my hand in the air. While I knew that technically it was too late to ask them if it was okay for Mona to join us, I still offered them a questioning glance as if to say without words, "Is it okay with you if she joins us?"

Both Kaia and Thomas responded to my look with a sort of shoulder-shrug-eyebrow-lift that seemed to say, "I guess since you already offered it in front of the whole class, it's okay."

"Good," Mrs. Yano said. "So everyone has a group now."

Mona looked at me with a smile and adjusted her glasses. I smiled back and nodded as if to say, "You're welcome." It's funny how much we say without even using any words.

Mrs. Yano handed out outlines for the project, and we spent the rest of the class going over the details, but my attention kept drifting. "Why didn't anyone want to be in group with Mona?" I asked myself. She was smart and knowledgeable about things and seemed to be pretty friendly and good-natured. She also seemed like the kind of kid who would be a hard worker. So why didn't the other kids want her in their group?

As the sound of the bell pulled me out of my thoughts, I realized that I had no clue what Mrs. Yano had just said about the project. Hopefully, with the help of the outline and my group mates, I would be okay.

As I gathered my books and got up to leave, Mona came up to me.

"Thanks for letting me into your group," she said in a sweet voice. "You know, I tried joining some other groups. I asked Susan, Debbie and Rachel. Then I asked Emily, and I asked Matt and Dale. And after that, I went up to Aaron and Steven, and even Billy, and they all said they already had groups. By the time I had asked all of them, Mrs. Yano was calling us back to our seats."

"Why do you think they didn't let you join their groups, Mona?" My question brought about a thoughtful look on Mona's face, and she adjusted her glasses as she contemplated what I had asked.

"Well," she said, "most of them told me they already had groups. So I guess that was why." But she did not seem particularly satisfied with her answer. "You know, Johnny, it's not the first time this sort of thing has happened to me. Kids often don't let me join in their groups in class, or at lunch or recess for that matter."

"Any idea why?" I asked.

Mona's expression shifted from thoughtful to slightly sad.

The Case of Monologuing Mona

"Not really. I try to be nice and friendly, but sometimes it seems like kids just don't want to be around me. So would you call that a social mystery, Johnny?"

"Genuine, one hundred percent, bona fide social mystery," I said.

"Do you think you could solve it?" Mona then asked.

"Well, I can't guarantee it, but I have a pretty good track record."

"Okay then," she said, reaching into her pocket and pulling out a neatly folded stack of bills. "It's a dollar a day plus expenses, right?" she confirmed, handing me a dollar.

"Yup. That's right. How did you know?" I asked.

"I know a lot of things, Johnny. I'm just not so sure about people sometimes," she said, her face taking on a twinge of sadness again.

"Well, let's see if we can work on that together, Mona. I'll get right on your case. Just do what you usually do, and we will figure it out."

We parted ways, and as I watched Mona walk down the hall and disappear into the distance, I thought about how I used to be. I used to be the kid who knew a lot about a lot of things but seemed to always be in the dark about people and why they acted the way they did. If I could figure it out, I'm sure Mona could, too. She was a really smart kid.

Lunch is often the best time of the day for gathering facts. It is a time when all the kids are interacting and there is minimal teacher interference, which means that the real social dynamics can show themselves.

"Social dynamics" are a mixture of all the spoken and unspoken social rules, all the different types of interactions between kids, all the attitudes, ideas and expressions plus loads of other social-type things that are a part of our interactions with each other. I often call these social dynamics the "social symphony," because it's like all the separate aspects of social relating come together to make a kind of social music. Sometimes when things are working well, the music is beautiful. But when things are not really working, the music is out of key or off beat.

Lunchtime always offers a wide variety of social symphonies, providing an observant social detective with lots of valuable clues. The only downside of gathering clues at lunchtime is that I don't get to hang out with my friends. But that is the life of a social detective, and fortunately my friends are very understanding.

It was a beautiful day and, as a result, lots of the kids were eating lunch in the grassy area just outside the cafeteria. I spotted Mona as she came out of the cafeteria with a hot lunch tray. Today they were serving some type of meat-like substance that bore a striking resemblance to the sea monster that took over New York in the black-and-white horror movie I had seen on television the previous week.

I crumpled my lunch sack between my fingers as I thought of the comparison. The crinkling sound was very reassuring. While my mom might not be the most creative lunch maker, it was comforting to know that I would never be pulling anything out of my lunch bag that looked as scary as some of the things that I see being scooped out of the huge cauldron-like pots in the cafeteria.

Mona walked to the middle of the grass area and paused, scanning the various groups of kids. She targeted a group of girls sitting in a circle, talking happily as they ate their lunches. Mona walked over to them. While I couldn't hear what she said, it seemed like she was asking if she could join them. The other girls exchanged glances and, after a pause, nodded to Mona and she sat down.

Body language says a lot, and the nods given to Mona seemed very telling. As a social detective, I am always looking closely at what people are communicating. Usually when someone is welcome in a group, the head nod is accompanied by an arm motion that invites the person in, not just with words or an affirmative head gesture but with the whole body.

Motioning to someone with your arms to come over is a powerful way of saying, "Hey, I want you here." But Mona did not get any arm waving. What Mona got was a chorus of shoulder shrugs to accompany the head nods of approval. I call that kind of gesture combination a "mixed body message." The kids' heads were saying, "Yes, you can sit down," but a shoulder shrug does not communicate "yes." It communicates, "I don't know," or maybe even, "I guess you can sit here if you really have to."

This was all very interesting, but I still didn't know why kids would be giving Mona a mixed body message like that. I could see what was happening, but I still didn't know why. I needed to look for more clues.

I sat down on the grass a little bit away from the group Mona was in. I discreetly pulled out my spy listening device, put in my earplugs and inconspicuously pointed the mic towards the group of girls. They were talking about music and how cute the singer of some new pop band was. They all laughed and giggled. Mona didn't say much, but she did join in the giggling.

The conversation soon switched to the strange brownish-gray lumps the cafeteria was dishing out to unsuspecting students.

"So what do you think is in that stuff?" Jacqueline asked.

"I think they use old gym socks to add flavor," Martha offered.

Everyone laughed as they took turns suggesting strange things the cafeteria workers might be using to make their mysterious food concoctions. Guesses ranged from moldy cheese to three-year-old taco meat, to a collection of rancid hair balls hacked up by a pack of wild cats.

The conversation was quite funny – much better than the blah blah blah of the typical girl talk about how cute some pop singer was. I found myself giggling and thinking up other strange possibilities for school cafeteria recipes.

Eventually, the girls' conversation moved on, and not surprisingly the next topic was fashion. Again Mona just smiled, sweetly contributing a well-timed giggle here and there. Her body language and facial expressions conveyed that she was paying attention. She nodded at the right times, looked at the person who was talking and laughed when something was funny.

As the girls chatted away, the conversation moved from topic to topic. The subject of Mrs. Reader's big English test that afternoon came up, and at the mention of that Mona was brought to life. The test was on the book *Charlotte's Web*, which the class had been assigned to read. Mona spoke for the first time since she had joined the group.

"I loved *Charlotte's Web*," she said. "It was such a great story." Her eyes twinkled with excitement as she described in detail her favorite parts of the story. Her voice was very animated and excited as she spoke. Mona was still describing her favorite parts of the story when the bell rang. She continued talking as the others gathered their things and joined the herd of kids slowly migrating back to class.

After everyone had left, Mona picked up her lunch tray and backpack and disappeared into the stream of class-bound students. I gathered up my gear, dived into the streams of kids myself and made my way to class. I was also in Mrs. Reader's English class and did not want to be late for the test.

Tuesday, 12:46 PM

"All right, everyone. I have a little surprise for you," Mrs. Reader announced. "As I'm sure you all know, today is test day. But we are going to do the test a little differently. Instead of the usual written test, this time we are going to do an oral test. The test will be in the form of a discussion in which you will all take turns answering questions about the book. And we are going to video tape the discussion and show it at open house so your parents will get to see you all in action."

Once again open house was taking over the school and making the teachers obsessed with finding creative ways to torture us, in order to entertain our parents. But I'd much rather be filmed than have to do another art project, so I was happy.

Just then, Phil Maker entered the class, video camera in hand. Phil is a fellow student who is set on becoming a famous Hollywood movie director before the age of 25. And I would say he is well on his way. Phil already has 17 homemade movies posted on YouTube and has volunteered as the school's multimedia aide, which means he gets to miss class to do things like set up overhead projectors and film campus events. And it seemed that today our class was the event to be filmed.

The Case of Monologuing Mona

Mrs. Reader opened her notebook. Phil nodded to confirm he was ready for action.

"Who can tell me about one of the main characters in the story?" Mrs. Reader asked.

A sea of hands went up. This was an easy question, and everyone jumped at it. Mrs. Reader called on Debbie.

But because this was a show for the parents and not just a simple question, Debbie had to stand up to answer. Debbie was very poised and carried herself well. She turned towards the camera and began to speak in a very cheery voice. "One of the main characters in the book was Charlotte," she said and then paused to see if there was a follow-up question.

"Why do you think she was a main character?" Mrs. Reader asked. "She was a main character because she played a very important role in the story."

"Can you tell us a little about Charlotte, Debbie?" Mrs. Reader asked as if she were a talk show host interviewing someone.

Debbie gave a very nice and to-the-point description of Charlotte.

"Very good. Thank you," Mrs. Reader said. Debbie smiled and seemed to take a little bow as she sat back down in her chair.

Mrs. Reader continued to ask the class questions about the book, and the kids continued to perform for the video camera. You could tell that Mona had read the book because her hand went up for every question the teacher asked. And each time she did not get called on, she seemed to get a little more agitated.

By the time Mrs. Reader had asked the fifth question, Mona could not contain herself any longer. She was bouncing in her seat and making a low-pitched "oh oh" type of grunt that got a little louder every time she was not picked.

Finally, Mrs. Reader called on her. "Okay, Mona, you seem ready for a question. Tell me what Wilber was worried about."

Mona almost jumped out of her seat. "Well, sure, I know that. You see, Wilber was a pig. A very special pig. When he was born, he was really small, but Fern took good care of him, so he got big and healthy. Fern fed him food and visited him every day. She loved animals. I love animals too. And Wilber, he was *sooo* sweet. But you see a farm … Well you know, on farms they eat animals and one day some of the animals started talking about the farmer and …"

"So, Mona, can you tell us what Wilber was worried about?" Mrs. Reader restated the question.

"Yeah sure, I was getting to that," Mona replied. "So Wilber, he was scared because, well, he was kind of a scared pig to begin with. Maybe that was because he was small when he was born, or maybe it was because he was taken away from his mom when he was little. You know little animals need their parents just like kids do, so that may be why he got worried sometimes …"

The Case of Monologuing Mona

"Mona, what was Wilber worried about in the story," Mrs. Reader repeated.

"Well, yeah, so in the story he had heard that the farmer was going to eat him. Some of the other animals had told him that, and that's why Charlotte was helping him. Charlotte really liked Wilber, and she told him not to worry. She came up with this great plan to help Wilber. One night when everyone was sleeping, she …"

"Thank you, Mona. You can have a seat now."

You could tell Mona was excited and wanted to keep going. It took her until the next kid started talking to sit down. She really seemed to love the book.

The questions kept coming, and the video kept rolling. I got to talk about Templeton the rat and how he helped to save Wilber's life. By the end of the class, everyone had had a chance to say something.

"Great job, everyone," Mrs. Reader said with a big smile on her face.

I have to admit that by the end, I was having a little trouble keeping my eyes open. I leaned over to Jeff who was sitting next to me. "At least this beats having to do another art project for open house," I whispered.

Jeff giggled. But within seconds of my saying that, Mrs. Reader announced that she wanted us all to do dioramas of our favorite scene from *Charlotte's Web*. Jeff looked at me and exploded with laughter. I could feel my face melting into a pained expression, which made Jeff laugh even harder.

"Nice," I said.

"That's the third diorama I've been assigned this week," Jeff commented.

"Yeah, but you like that kind of thing. I, on the other hand, find those kinds of projects a form of child torture."

The bell rang, and I made a few notes in my detective notebook. I was definitely gathering some important clues about Mona. But I needed more facts.

Wednesday, 4:02 PM

I knocked on the door of Kaia's house and waited. Kaia, Thomas, Mona and I were meeting to work on our group project for Mrs. Reader's class. Kaia had volunteered to host our meeting. The door opened, and there she was with a big smile on her face. She has long brown hair with blondish streaks in it, and when she smiles like she was doing right now, her whole face lights up.

The Case of Monologuing Mona

Kaia is definitely one of the cool kids in school, but unlike some kids who let their popularity go to their heads, Kaia remains sweet and friendly to everyone.

"Hey, Johnny. Come on in. Thomas is already here," she said.

I joined them in the living room, and we all greeted each other. Thomas high-fived me and offered the classic guy greeting of "What's up, Johnny?"

I responded to his "What's up?" with "Not much. What's up with you?" to which Thomas did not really respond.

Often the "What's up?" is said not as much as a real question to which you expect a response, as another version of "Hey."

In fact, if you really responded to that kind of a "What's up?" with a detailed explanation of what was going on with you, people might think you were strange. But it is tricky because sometimes when people ask you "What's up?" they really mean it as a question and not just as a way of saying "Hello." So you have to read the situation and look for all the clues to see what kind of a "What's up?" someone is asking you.

Just then the doorbell rang and Kaia disappeared, returning a moment later with Mona.

"Hi, Mona," I said with a smile on my face.

"Hi, Johnny," she said returning the smile.

"What's going on, Mona?" Thomas asked, giving Mona one of those laid-back, guy type of head nods.

"Oh, things have been pretty busy lately. I have some relatives who came into town to visit, and we've been doing a lot of family stuff. Of course, my relatives want to go sightseeing, which is fun. But, you know, there is so much work to do right now in school that it's hard to make time for everything. We did go to the museum of history last weekend, and they actually had an exhibit on the Civil War …"

"Speaking of which, we should probably get started on our report," I said, trying to get our meeting underway. It was nice to socialize, but the truth was I wanted to get home and have some time to read the new detective novel I'd just got.

Kaia began by suggesting we break down the project into parts and decide who would do what.

I proposed we start by dividing the writing part up into sections. The first part would be about what led up to the war, and the second part could be about the war itself. Thomas suggested we divide the diorama task into making people and making scenery.

I quickly volunteered to do some of the writing.

The Case of Monologuing Mona

"I'll make the army guys," Thomas said. It was a pretty sure bet that Thomas would volunteer for that part. He was the artsy type, not so much the wordsy writer type.

Kaia said she would write about what led up to the war itself.

"Sounds good to me. Then I'll write about the actual war," I said.

That left Mona. "I'll do the scenery then," Mona said in a cheery and agreeable voice.

She continued, "You know, when I was at the museum the other day, they showed a lot of scenes from the Civil War. They showed a lot of houses from back then as well. I can make some houses to go with the scenery."

"That sounds great," Thomas said.

"Yeah, the houses back then were really pretty. And did you know that back then people usually had a lot of land to build their houses on? That's because there were not as many people back then. Oh, and at the museum they showed all the outfits people wore and all the weapons they used.

"Did you know that they used muskets, which are these really old kinds of rifles that shoot these round metal balls instead of bullets? And the soldiers could only shoot one at a time, and then they had to reload. They had to put gunpowder in the gun, and then they packed it with a stick and..."

"That's interesting, Mona," I said. "So you do the scenery and …"

"Yeah, it is really interesting how difficult they had it back then. Did you know that Abraham Lincoln … blah blah? He thought that … blah blah blah blah, and when he … blah … was president, he blah blah blah, and the blah blah blah was blah, even when blah blah blah and blah and blah and …"

It was the strangest thing. I stared at Mona and really tried to listen to what she was saying, but it was as if she was speaking a foreign language. Everything she said sounded like "blah blah blah."

I found myself falling into a sort of hypnotic trance as she spoke. Every blah that came out of her mouth made my eyes feel a little bit heavier. I had to force myself to break my gaze before I became completely hypnotized and fell asleep.

I looked at Kaia and then at Thomas. They both looked back at me with an almost imperceptible grin on their faces. They were not mean looks. They were looks that seemed to convey a mix of amusement, irritation and uncertainty about how to handle to situation.

Mona didn't seem to notice that we weren't looking at her any more. She just kept talking away.

It was at that moment it all became clear to me. I snapped out of my hypnotic trance, and the solution to Mona's mystery flashed in my mind like a bolt of lightning. I took out my detective notebook and made my notes while Mona continued her blah blah blahing.

When I was done taking notes, it dawned on me that I was the one who'd invited Mona into our group. It was my doing and my responsibility. So it seemed only fair that I take charge of the situation.

"Mona," I said in a firm but friendly voice.

Mona had been getting increasingly more excited as she spoke and did not seem to hear me when I called her name.

"Mona," I said again, a little louder this time, and I added a slight arm gesture to get her attention. "I think we should move on and finish planning the project."

"Oh, yeah. Sure thing, Johnny," she said in a voice that was still excited but also very agreeable.

With some structure and a little effort to keep Mona in check, we got through the rest of the project planning pretty quickly and efficiently. The meeting ended up being a success for everyone. And it was a double success for me. Not only did I get out of doing an art project, I also solved another social mystery.

Can You Solve the Case of Monologuing Mona?

Here are some questions that might help you in solving the case:

- How would you describe the mystery?

- What are the facts in this case?

- How would you make sense of the facts?

- What are the biggest clues?

- What does Mona see as the problem?

- What do you think Johnny would see as the problem?

- What clues did Johnny find to help him solve the case?

- Why do you think the kids did not really want to be in a group with Mona?

- What did you think about Mona's answer to Mrs. Reader's question?

- What feedback did Mrs. Reader offer that gave a clue about what Mona was having difficulty with?

- What were Kaia's, Thomas' and Johnny's reactions when Mona was talking?

- Why did Johnny start feeling hypnotized when Mona was talking?

- Do you think you would be friends with Mona? Why?

- What social remedies would you offer to Mona?

- How would you test out your social remedies to see if they were working?

 # Cracking
the Case

Friday, 8:02 AM

I had emailed Mona and asked her to meet at the library
Friday before school to discuss her case. She was there
right on time, with a big smile and a cheery disposition. I
had reserved one of the library media rooms the day before
and, after greeting each other, Mona and I worked our way
through the maze of book-lined shelves that stood between us
and the entrance to the media center.

I opened the door, flipped the light on and sat down at one of
the many metal chairs that surrounded the round table in the
middle of the room. Mona followed my lead and sat in the
chair just to my right.

I adjusted my chair a little so I was facing Mona. "So," I
began, "I think I've found the answer to your mystery."

"That's great, Johnny. So what did you find?" she asked, with a look of anticipation on her face.

I thought for a minute before I spoke. As a social detective, you are often in a position of having to tell people things about themselves that are not the most flattering. Sometimes, with kids like Billy Bullington, that's pretty easy to do. In fact, it can feel good on occasion to let it rip and let the other person know all the things he or she is doing to annoy others.

Usually, the kids whose social mysteries I help to solve are nice, good kids who are just missing something. They usually don't mean any harm and just want to get along with others.

Mona is definitely one of those types of kids. So the challenge was to find a way to let her know what she needed to work on, without it coming across as critical or judgmental.

"Well," I said, after my pause to think about how to present my findings in the best way. "Why don't we start by taking a look at a clip from the video we made in English class yesterday to see if we can notice some of the clues together?"

I pulled out the video I'd convinced Phil to let me borrow and plugged it into the video machine in the room. I had cued it up ahead of time to the part where April was telling the class about the things Charlotte wrote in her web, and how the humans responded to it. Her answer was clear and to the point, with just the right amount of detail.

The Case of Monologuing Mona

When April was finished, I asked Mona what she thought of April's answer.

"It was very nice," Mona replied. "She did a very good job on it. You could tell she had read the story. And I like the dress she wore, too. She always dresses really nice and is really friendly. The other day …"

"Okay, Mona," I said, jumping in and interrupting her a little, in order to move forward. "So, now let's take a look at your response." I rolled the tape, and we watched together.

When Mona's segment finished, I asked her what she thought.

"Well, I was kind of nervous. You know I get nervous a lot when I have to talk in front of people. But I loved *Charlotte's Web* so that made me feel excited, too."

"I could definitely see that you were excited. How would you compare the length of your response to April's?" I asked.

Mona paused and gazed into space for a moment, thinking about my question. "I'm not sure, Johnny. I guess mine was probably longer."

"I think that one of the important clues to help solve your social mystery has to do with the length of your responses. One of the things I noticed, Mona, is that you frequently give very long answers to questions. And often your answers seem to contain much more information than what was called for in the question.

"Did you notice that in your response to what Wilber was worried about, you talked about things like when Wilber was born and how Fern liked animals and how you like animals?"

"Yeah. It was a great story, and there is so much to say," Mona said.

"That's true, Mona, but one thing that helps when we are with other people is to listen to what others are asking us and make sure we respond to them. Did you notice that Mrs. Reader had to interrupt you and repeat her question to you a few times?"

"Uh, no, I didn't notice that," Mona said, with a slightly concerned look on her face.

"I've noticed that I have also had to interrupt you a number of times, Mona. I don't like interrupting people, but sometimes it felt that if I didn't jump in, you might keep talking for a long time and go off in a completely different direction than where I was trying to go."

"Really? When did you feel you had to do that?" Mona asked with a sense of genuine curiosity that let me know she was open to what I was telling her.

"Do you remember a little while ago when I asked you what you thought of April's answer?"

"Sure. Of course, it was just a minute ago," she said.

"I had to interrupt you because, after you answered my question, you started talking about how you liked April's dress and how she is a nice person. I felt that, if I had not interrupted you, you might have gone on talking for a long time, and we wouldn't have any time left to crack your case before school started.

"And do you remember the other day at Kaia's house, how I had to interrupt you when you started talking about Abraham Lincoln so we could finish talking about the project?"

Mona looked at me as I spoke, her eyes widened a little, and her eyebrows turned up slightly. "I guess when I think back, I can see how you might have needed to do that," she said in a voice that seemed a little quivery, as if she was trying to be open to what I was saying, while still feeling a little bad hearing it.

"Mrs. Reader had to interrupt you too," I said, trying to be as gentle as I could, while still giving Mona the feedback she needed to crack the case.

"Here, let's take another look at the video," I said as I rewound the tape and played back the part where Mrs. Reader had to interrupt Mona and restate the question. I let it play to the end of Mona's answer where Mrs. Reader had to interrupt Mona once again to get her to stop talking.

"You know, Johnny, when I think about it, it seems like people interrupt me like that a lot. I think I was really excited, and I had a lot to say about the story," she said, fiddling with the rim of her glasses as she spoke.

"I can understand that, Mona. But sometimes when we don't respond to what someone asks us in a way that is short and to the point, the other person feels as if we are not paying attention and listening to what they are asking.

"If you asked me what I ate for breakfast, and I started telling you about all the things I liked to eat and what I did in the mornings, you might think I was not really responding to what you asked. And responding quickly, clearly and concisely to others is a very important part of being a good friend. When you respond quickly, clearly and concisely, it helps people to know that you are interested in them and paying attention to what they say."

"I was responding to Mrs. Reader's question, Johnny. I just added some other points that I thought were interesting."

"I can see that, Mona. But part of how we show others we are connected to them in a conversation is by staying on the main topic when we talk. The main topic is the central idea that is being talked about. Do you remember when we met at Kaia's house the other day? At one point we were talking about how we were going to divide up the project.

"The main topic at that point was the project. When we were talking about that, you did respond briefly to the topic, when you said you would do the scenery. But then you started talking about how hard it was back in those days and about Abraham Lincoln. While sometimes it's okay to drift smoothly from the main topic, it can be a problem if we move away from the main topic before we've really responded to it, and before the group we are a part of has finished discussing that topic.

"It's also important to be aware of how interested others are in what we are saying. Did you notice that when you switched subjects the other day and started talking about Abraham Lincoln, our eyes got a little glazed over, and we even stopped looking at you while you were talking?"

Mona paused again, trying to recall our meeting. "I don't remember that, Johnny," she said with a look of concentration on her face that showed she was genuinely trying to take everything I was saying in. "I do remember being really excited about the project and the museum and Abraham Lincoln."

"I could tell you were excited, Mona. But it's important to read your audience. What I mean by that is it's important to try to determine if others are also interested in what you are talking about."

"How do you do that, Johnny?"

"Facial expression and body language give you a lot of that kind of information. You want to ask yourself questions like, 'Does the other person's face look interested?' 'Is she looking at me or looking other places?' 'Is he nodding his head in response to what I'm saying, or is he sitting really still or even slumped over a little?'

"Those are a few questions you can ask yourself. It's also important to be aware of whether or not others are participating in what you are talking about, or whether you are just giving a monologue."

"What's a monologue, Johnny?"

"A monologue is a long speech by one person that does not allow for anyone else to speak. Monologues are never good in conversations with friends. People usually get really bored when someone is talking for too long and they don't get to interact at all," I explained.

"When I'm talking about something I'm really interested in," said Mona, "I think I could probably talk for a very long time. I like talking about all the little details. But I always imagined that others would be as excited and interested as I was and that they would enjoy hearing about the subject as much as I was enjoying talking about it. So how do I avoid doing a monologue when I'm really excited about something?"

"Well, the first thing you want to do is notice if you are staying on the topic or talking about other things. If you are staying on the main topic, it is less likely that you will get into a long, drawn-out monologue. You also want to be careful not to give too many details. Too many details are a sure-fire way to make people lose interest. If you try to keep in mind that you want to give people a summary of things, rather than giving them all the little details, it will help you avoid getting lost in too many details.

"Monologues are usually pretty long, but if you're staying on track and don't give too many details, you will be less likely to slip into a long monologue."

"When I'm excited about something, Johnny, I tend to forget about time."

"That's true for all of us, Mona. But if you make it a point to be aware of how long you are talking, it will make it easier to notice when you are going on too long. And you can always glance down at your watch when you start talking and then look back to see how much time has passed.

"Another thing you can do, if you are on a topic you really like and you want to keep talking about it, is to ask others their opinions and thoughts on the subject. Get them talking about it, too. That way you won't be monologuing. You will be interacting, which makes it interesting for everyone, not just the person talking. But if you try to get others involved in the topic you are interested in and they don't say much, and their body language tells you they are not really into it, you should probably try to find a different subject that is interesting for everyone."

"Sometimes it's hard, Johnny," said Mona, "because the things I'm interested in other kids often don't care about. I love learning and school. I love finding out facts about things like the weather and geography and science and history. And I love reading books. But I'm not really sure what other kids are interested in."

"Well, I'd say you might want to do something like joining the science club or maybe starting a history club or a book club. I know there are other kids who share your interests. You just haven't found them yet. As for not knowing what other kids are interested in, maybe you could try to find out. It could be a sort of science project for you to research what other kids are into. Then you could make sure to balance out conversation with things that others like as well."

"Are you saying I should be a social detective like you, Johnny, and try to solve the mystery of what other kids find interesting?"

"That's exactly what I am saying. You catch on quickly!" I said with a big smile on my face.

"So how do I do that?" Mona asked.

"If you keep your eyes and ears open for clues, I'm sure you will find lots of facts about what excites others. Listen to what they talk about, and look to see what things they respond to with excitement. And asking questions is one of the best things you can do to find out what others are interested in. Not only will asking questions give you a lot of important clues about others, it will also keep you from talking too much yourself.

The Case of Monologuing Mona

"If you're asking questions, you give others the opportunity to talk. And the best part of asking questions is that by asking others about themselves and their interests and opinions, you are showing them that you are interested in them. And showing others you're interested in them is a very important part of being a good friend."

Mona was quiet. I was quiet. We had covered all the main points I had hoped to cover, and there were two minutes left before the morning bell would ring.

Mona was really open to all the feedback I gave her, and as a social detective who has worked with loads of kids, I knew that being open and curious about things was one of the most important parts of making positive change.

After a long, reflective pause, Mona brought her eyes to mine. "So what got you interested in becoming a social detective, Johnny?"

This was a great question for so many reasons. It was a change in the main topic, but it was a change at just the right time. We had finished discussing what we had been talking about, and there was even a pause to make it clear that we were ready to move on. In addition, her question was related to the previous topic, so it made the transition smooth and relevant.

Her question could help her understand another person's interests, just as we had been talking about. And it showed interest in other people's thoughts and ideas. Most of all, for me, it was a question that I loved to answer.

A river of words approached my lips and got ready to rush out of my mouth and flow with all the details of how I came to be Johnny Multony, social detective. But before those words had the chance to tell their tale, the bell rang, summoning us to first period.

"That will have to be a tale for another time," I said to Mona.

 "I look forward to listening to it some time, Johnny," Mona said with a sweet smile on her face and a genuine twinkle in her eye. "Thanks for all your help."

"It was my pleasure, Mona. Let me know how it goes."

The case was officially solved, and I felt hopeful that Mona would use the tools we had talked about to make things better in her life. What more could a social detective ask for?

Chapter 8

It's My Game, and I'll Win if I Want To: The Case of the Girl Who Struck out While Hitting a Home Run

The entire school was buzzing with excitement. Yesterday our baseball team, the Chipmunks, beat the Hawks, putting our school in first place in our division. This allowed us to move up to the regional baseball playoffs, which start next week. What made the win extra sweet was the fact that the Hawks were the Chipmunks' biggest rivals.

Yes, it's true. Our school mascot, who is supposed to instill fear and a powerful sense of intimidation in all teams who dare to face us in the arena of competition, is a tiny, cute, would-never-hurt-a-fly chipmunk. Who came up with the idea of a chipmunk as our mascot I don't know, but I have always imagined it was someone's sweet old grandmother.

Part of the reason why the Hawks are such big rivals is that they always make jokes about how they are gonna swoop down and grab us in their talons, then feed us to their young. At the games between our schools, they paint big pictures of hawks carrying scared little chipmunks in their claws and wave their works of art in the air to taunt us.

If I ever get the opportunity to pick a mascot, I guarantee it will be something much bigger and higher on the food chain than a chipmunk. But our little old Chipmunks had definitely swooped down on those Hawks yesterday, with a devastating score of Chipmunks 9: Hawks 4.

Our school hasn't made it to the playoffs in years, so this was a huge victory. The cafeteria staff joined in the celebration by serving the traditional baseball game meal of hot dogs and French fries. They even made little cakes shaped like baseballs for dessert.

Usually I do everything I can to stay far away from the school cafeteria cuisine. But these were official ball park hotdogs bought especially in honor of the victory, so I thought I'd make an exception and partake in the lunch time festivities.

I took my tray and worked my way through the crowd of kids to my usual lunch table. Already sitting at the table was Sora Loosoreea. She looked miserable. Her head was resting in her hands, her shoulders hunched over as she stared off into space, looking like she was about to cry.

The Case of the Girl Who Struck out While Hitting a Home Run

As I sat down across from her, she brought her eyes to meet mine. Without the typical friendly greeting one offers others, Sora jumped right in and got to the point.

"This is your detective office, right?" she blurted out, as she pulled out a wad of money from her pocket. "How much is it gonna cost me to hire you?"

I was caught a little off guard. Not only was there no hello, no small talk, there was not even an introduction to her problem to see if it was something I could help her with.

I responded to Sora's question with uncertainty in my voice. "When I take a case, you know … uh, if it's a case that I can help someone on, and I need to hear about it first … Well, in situations like that I, uh, well, I charge a dollar a day plus expenses."

Sora removed a dollar bill from her wad of money and pushed it towards me on the table. "I seriously need your help, Johnny. And I need it like yesterday!"

I left the bill on the table. Accepting it would mean taking the case, and I never take on a case before I know what it involves.

"Tell me what's going on, Sora," I said in my most professional social detective voice and then took a big, delicious bite of my hot dog.

"Our first playoff game is Monday," she said.

"I know. I would think you would be excited about that, Sora, considering you are one of the team's all-stars. I don't think we would have made it this far if it wasn't for your excellent ball playing," I added.

"Well, apparently the coach doesn't see it that way, because he just passed out the line-up for the first playoff game, and he's not playing me." Sora's voice crackled, expressing anger and sadness at the same time. "I can't understand why he wouldn't play me, Johnny. I struck out 10 kids at bat in the last game and was responsible for 9 other outs as well. I also hit a grand slam home run, which won the game. I thought I was a shoe-in for most valuable player this year. And then this! I just can't understand why Coach Ity would not play me in the game."

"Why wouldn't Coach play you, Sora? I mean, maybe it was a mistake. Did you ask him about it?"

"When I asked him why he wasn't playing me, he told me that if I didn't get it by now, I would never get it. And then he just walked away. Sports are my life, Johnny, and baseball is the thing I want to do more than anything. I just don't get it. So do you think you can help me?" she asked, her voice still crackling with emotion.

"This definitely is a social mystery, Sora. You are one of the best players on the team. I can't understand why the coach wouldn't play you."

I picked up the dollar bill Sora had placed on the table. "I'll take the case, Sora. And we need to get on it right away."

I had a personal interest in this one. I wanted our team to win the playoffs. That would mean a school trophy and a chance to play in the championship series. And I knew that Sora, who truly was one of our school's best players, could help us reach that goal. Why would the coach not want to play her in such an important game? That was a question I was determined to find an answer to.

"So what should I do, Johnny?" Sora asked.

"Just do what you always do, Sora, and I'll take care of the rest. We will get to the bottom of this one."

Hearing my words, Sora let a smile slip through the sadness that had enveloped her face. She got up, put her baseball cap on and walked away. As I finished my lunch, I planned out the best way to proceed. I decided that the first thing to do would be to get a look at Sora in action. So I decided to stake out the baseball practice that afternoon.

Wednesday, 4:03 PM

I set up my stake-out near a bush that was perfectly positioned between third base and the dugout. I brought my listening device and digital recorder, along with my trusty notebook. I had just got a fancy adaptor that could connect my digital recorder with my special spy listening device. So not only could I hear a whisper from 200 feet away, I could record it as well. This could help tremendously in some of my cases.

I had to be careful because such technology in the wrong hands can cause all kinds of trouble. I have special permission from the principal to use my spy devices, but hate to think what someone who was messed up could do with a device like this. They could spy on conversations – not to help but to hurt.

One of the mysteries I have yet to fully solve is how some people can be so mean to others. For example, there are kids who tell other kids' secrets just to hurt them. They gossip and say mean things, and even make up lies about others just to be hurtful.

Why? Why would people do that? Do they think they are being cool by hurting others? Do they think other kids want to be friends with them because they are good at stabbing other kids in the back? Of course, we don't want that.

So why would kids do that? Maybe they have been hurt and are not smart enough to do anything else but take things out on others. Maybe they feel so bad about themselves and are not strong enough to take responsibility for their own feelings, so they try to make others feel worse instead

The truth is I don't know exactly why kids would act so mean. It's still a mystery to me. But it is a mystery I would have to think more about at a later time, because right now I was on a case.

The Case of the Girl Who Struck out While Hitting a Home Run

Coach Ity appeared on the field, followed by a stream of excited-looking players. I brought my focus away from the mystery of mean kids and back to the task at hand. I quickly pulled out some school books to use as my cover and keep people from getting suspicious about what I was doing there. As far as others would know, I was just doing my homework. The team members started throwing balls back and forth to one another while they waited for the coach to start things up.

It was clear that Mr. Ity was excited about moving to the playoffs. His voice was louder than usual, but you could tell by the music in his voice that it was an excited loud, not an irritated loud.

"Today we are going to have a practice game," he said in his big, booming voice. He split the team up and assigned everyone positions to play in the practice game. Sora was one of the few girls on the team, but she was by far one of the best players. She was an excellent pitcher as well as being great at first base.

But today Mr. Ity had her playing right field. When he announced Sora's position, she let out a loud huffing sound, threw her hands, glove and all, up over her head, then turned and walked out into right field. It was clear to everyone that she was disappointed with having to play that position. Mr. Ity paused briefly and shook his head in response to Sora's huffing and hand waving. But he quickly went back to assigning field positions and batting line-ups.

As the game started, there was a charge of excitement in all the players. Even though this was practice, it seemed like everyone was playing as if it was the championship game. Nick was pitching for Sora's team, and he was on fire.

"Strike," said the umpire as Nick ripped one past home plate.

Again, "strrrrr-ike!" came out of the umpire's mouth in classic umpire style, as Tommy swung and missed the second pitch.

Nick wound up again and fired the ball towards home plate.

"Ball!" called the umpire, waving his arms to indicate to anyone who could not hear his big umpire voice that it was indeed a ball.

Then again, "Ball!" announced the umpire, holding up two fingers on each hand to indicate that there were now two balls and two strikes.

"Come on, Nick. Get it together!" exclaimed Sora from the outfield.

Nick ignored her and pitched one right down the center.

Tommy clobbered it, sending one right over the third baseman's head, enabling him to get on base safely.

Normally at a ball game, you know who you are rooting for. But this was my team playing against my team so I was kinda rooting for them all. I was excited when Nick threw a perfect strike, and

I was excited when Tommy clobbered the ball and got on first. Their skills would serve our team well in the playoffs next week.

Sora did not seem too happy for Tommy, however, and I noticed her throwing her glove on the ground when he made it to first base without getting out.

Susan was up to bat next and, after a strike and a ball, she nailed the ball just over the first baseman's head. Sora fielded the ball, but instead of throwing it to the second baseman, she ran over and tagged Tommy out at second base.

In the process, Stewart, who was playing second base, had to jump out of the way so Sora would not bump into him. But she did get the out.

Sean was up next. Nick took him out quickly. "Strike one, strike two, strike three," called the umpire as Sean swung and missed on all three pitches.

Next up was Danny, who smacked the first pitch, sending it high up into center field. I saw Sora running from right field to center, but Brandon, who was playing center field, was all over it. He snapped up the ball before it found its way to the ground, giving Sora's team their third out.

The teams switched, and Sora and her teammates headed for the dugout. Sora was the seventh player up to bat. Not a great batting position for someone like Sora, who was an excellent hitter. She had an excellent batting average and was one of the fastest runners on the team. Playing right field and batting seventh was not because of her skills at fielding and hitting.

By the time Sora was up to bat, her team had already scored two runs; there was one out and the bases were loaded. Sora had a laser-like focus as she stepped up to the plate and took her practice swing.

The pitcher wound up and threw … "Ball!" called the umpire.

Sora shifted on her feet, readying herself for the next pitch … The ball flew across the plate …"Strike!" called the umpire, as he motioned with his arm and held up a finger on each hand.

"What!" exclaimed Sora. "That was way out there!" she yelled in an irritated voice.

I saw Mr. Ity shake his head again.

The next ball came straight down the middle. Sora hit it, a line drive right between first and second base. The right fielder pounced on the ball and threw it to the catcher, who tagged David as he slid into home plate.

"Out!" called the umpire.

It was a great play by everyone. Great hit, great fielding, great slide by David, and great tag by the catcher.

Next up to bat was Eric, who, unfortunately, tipped the ball, popping it up in the air, in the perfect position for the catcher to snatch it up, giving them their third out of the inning.

Sora went back to the dugout to get her glove and, as she passed by Eric, she pushed his shoulder and said "Nice one" in an irritated voice.

Sora's team did not do so well in the field the next inning. Two base hits and a home run gave the other team the lead.

I could see that with each hit, missed out and man on base, Sora seemed to get more and more agitated. She would mumble to herself and make comments about the umpire's calls. When Kyle hit a home run, she threw her glove down again and let out a groan so loud that everyone could hear. I saw Coach Ity look in the direction of Sora's groans and once again shake his head. Sora continued mumbling and making comments to herself during the rest of the inning. At one point Stewart, who was playing second base, turned around and told Sora to shut up.

Another time during the inning, when a ball was hit straight towards the second baseman, Sora ran from right field and jumped in front of Stewart to catch it. Then she tagged out the runner, who had started to run from second to third base.

It was a double play, and Sora had shown speed, agility and skill in single-handedly getting two outs at once. But that is not all she had shown. She had shown enough for me to say for sure that the case had been cracked. I turned off my recorder, put away my gear and my detective notebook, and simply watched the rest of the practice.

As I watched, I thought about all the things that go into being a good athlete. Then I thought about Sora's qualities and tried to think about what I would do if I were Coach Ity. And while I worried about how our team would do without her, I had to admit that if I were the coach I might not play her either.

But there was still time. If we acted quickly, there was a chance that Sora could make things right before the playoffs – if she was willing, open and able to take a good hard look at herself and make some changes.

When the practice ended, I moved over towards Sora.

"Hey, Johnny," she greeted me.

"Hey, Sora. I think I have the answer to your mystery."

Her face brightened. "Really, Johnny? That was quick."

"I'll wait for you outside the locker room; we can talk then, okay?"

"Yeah, sure thing, Johnny. I'll be quick." She grabbed her gear and took off towards the locker room.

Normally, I would have waited until the next day to talk to my client about a case. I usually like to have some time to contemplate the cases I'm working on. But there was no time to spare, and I had a personal interest in this. I wanted our team to have the best chance possible at the playoffs, and that meant having players who had all the necessary qualities. Even though Sora was not being a good player, I believed that with a little work she could become a most valuable player for her team.

Can You Solve the case of the Girl Who Struck out While Hitting a Home Run?

Here are some questions that might help you in solving the case:

- How would you describe the mystery?

- What are the facts in this case?

- How would you make sense of the facts?

- What are the biggest clues?

- What does Sora see as the problem?

- What do you think Johnny would see as the problem?

- What clues did Johnny find to help him solve the case?

- Why did Johnny think Sora was not being a good player for the team?

- What are the things you think go into being a good athlete?

- What do you think about Sora's reactions at the game?

- Why do you think Sora reacted at the game the way she did?

- What effect do you think her reactions had on others?

- Why did Johnny say he would do the same thing Coach Ity did?

- Do you think you would be friends with Sora? Why?

- What social remedies would you offer to Sora?

- How would you test out your social remedies to see if they are working?

Cracking the Case

Wednesday, 5:42 PM

Sora came out of the girls' locker room, wet hair flopping as she walked, gym bag slung over her shoulder. She had the perfect athlete's strut. Even if you had never seen her play ball, you could tell by the way she walked that she was agile and coordinated.

Some people walk in a way that lets you know they are not comfortable in their bodies. But Sora's strut made it clear that she was naturally comfortable in her body. Her motions were flowing, not jerky or awkward. And there was confidence in each step she took.

The Case of the Girl Who Struck out While Hitting a Home Run

The way we move our bodies is an important part of body language. And body language communicates a lot to others.

I was sitting on a table just outside the gym, my feet planted firmly on the bench below. Normally, we would be told off for sitting on the table rather than the bench, but the yard patrol was long gone, and it was so much more comfortable to sit on the table, so I took advantage of the situation.

Sora came over, threw her bag on the bench and sat down, cross-legged and facing me, at the other end of the table. Her posture was straight, but there was still a relaxed sense to her. Even the way she sat seemed cool and comfortable.

She stared at me for a moment. I met her gaze and gave a slight smile. The nature of our meeting was not happy-go-lucky, and Sora's facial expression and body language communicated that she was not in a light and playful mood. So I made sure my smile was not so big that it failed to match the weight and feeling of Sora's mood and the situation at hand. It was just big enough to convey friendliness.

"Right field!" she blurted out. "Coach played me in right field! I'm one of the best players on the team. I even thought I might get the Most Valuable Player Award this year. And he's got me playing right field!"

It's often difficult for a social detective to find just the right place to jump in and start sharing findings with a client, but Sora had given me the perfect opening.

"What do you think makes a player valuable, Sora?" I asked as a way of smoothly shifting our conversation to my findings.

"You know, if you play well. And I always play well," she replied.

"What does playing well involve?" I asked, hoping to get a little more of a detailed answer from Sora. I wanted to get a sense of what she saw as valuable qualities in team members.

"You know, Johnny. Someone who plays well can hit the ball a good percentage of the time. They have some control over where they hit the ball, which helps decrease the chances that the other team will catch it and get them out. Also, a good player can run fast, throw fast and catch the ball. Stuff like that."

"Those are all part of being a good player, Sora. You're right. But there are some other things involved in being a Most Valuable Player that are just as important, if not more important than the ones you mentioned."

I paused to observe Sora's reaction to what I had said. Her face looked puzzled. Her eyebrows were raised, and her head tilted slightly to the side, as if the angle would help her brain make better sense of what I was saying. It was clear from her expression that she had no idea what I was talking about. She had no clue what the other important aspects of being a good player were.

After a long pause, Sora finally said, "What are you talking about?"

"You described someone's skill with the basic tasks involved in playing baseball. Skill at those basic tasks is an important part of being a good player. And if we were talking about a sport like tennis or golf, or even one-on-one basketball, that would probably be a sufficient definition of skill. But baseball involves much more than skill with the basic tasks of the game. Do you know why that is, Sora?" I asked.

"I have no idea what you're talking about, Johnny. It's all about the skill as far as I'm concerned. Play hard. Play flawlessly. Win the game," Sora declared in a voice that revealed her strong conviction as well as her total cluelessness.

"I'd say there's more than that, Sora. Baseball is a sport where the goal is for the team to win. Baseball is a team sport and, because of that, it's not enough just to be thinking about your own game. You need to be thinking about the team's game."

"I'm always thinking about the team, Johnny. And for the team to win, the individuals on the team need to be playing well, right?"

"That's definitely true, Sora. But my point is that playing well on a team involves not just your own personal skill, but also your skill as a team player. So my question for you is this: How would you rate yourself as a team player?"

"I've never really thought about that," she replied honestly.

"Based on what I saw today in practice, I can see how you might never have thought about that before. As an individual you played hard, and you played flawlessly. But as a team player, I'd say you were, well … You were the least valuable player on the team."

"What's that supposed to mean?" Sora blurted out defensively.

"I imagine you're used to Coach Ity being straight with you about how you're playing. So I'm gonna be straight with you, too. While you are great at the basic skills of the game, you're a pretty bad team player, and your sportsmanship, well, it sucks."

It is important to note that, for many kids, I would be much gentler in the way I shared my findings. But Sora was a tough kid, and she seemed to pay more attention to toughness. So I did my best to speak in a way that Sora could appreciate and be receptive to.

For another kid, talking the way I did to Sora would have been the worst way to get my point across. But for Sora it was the best way, I thought. Good communicators don't just speak well. They adjust the way they speak to match the person they are talking to, so that the other person can absorb what they are saying.

"So you are saying I'm a bad sport?" Sora asked in an irritated voice.

"Let's break it down a little. I'll give you some examples that might help to make my point clearer. Being a team player is an important part of good sportsmanship, so let's start there. Good team players try to reach the goal of winning the game by working cooperatively with the other members of their team. They compete with the other team, but they cooperate with the members of their own team.

"Today at practice, you did an excellent job of competing with the other team. But when it came to working together with your own teammates, your game was way off.

"Do you remember in the first inning when Tommy hit the ball and you fielded it? Instead of throwing the ball to Stewart, you ran over to tag Tommy out yourself. Stewart had to jump out of the way so you wouldn't run into him.

"And later on in the game, you jumped right in front of Stewart to get a ball that was coming directly to him and then, instead of throwing the ball to Stewart so he could tag the runner out, you chased the runner down and tagged him out."

"Yeah, and I made a double play all by myself!" Sora exclaimed defensively.

"I know you made a double play all by yourself. But the point is that baseball is a team sport, not one you play all by yourself. You need to work with your teammates, not just play the game on your own. How do you think Stewart felt when you stole the play from him both those times?"

"I didn't think of it as stealing the play from him," Sora replied. "I just thought of it as trying to win the game."

"That may be how you saw it, Sora, but as a team player, it is important to think about how others might be seeing your actions. And I'm telling you that others would see your stealing the play from Stewart as you being a bad team player and trying to take all the glory for yourself."

"I never looked at it like that," Sora said in a voice that was now less defensive and more thoughtful.

"And then there is the issue of your attitude towards your fellow teammates when they were not flawless in their performance. You told Nick to 'get it together' in an irritated, harsh voice when he pitched two balls. And when Eric struck out, you said, 'Nice one' in a really nasty, critical way, and you pushed his shoulder aggressively."

"I wasn't that nasty," Sora countered.

At that comment, I pulled out my digital recorder and played for her how she had acted towards Nick and Eric, as well as a few other choice moments from the practice.

Sora looked surprised.

"Sometimes we don't realize the way we are saying things," I commented.

"They weren't playing well enough, Johnny, and it made me mad. Sometimes I get really irritated at things like that."

"Those guys are on your team, Sora. And that's not the way to treat your fellow teammates. That is the way you alienate people and make it so they don't want to play with you. I gotta tell you, Sora, with the way you acted out there today, I'm surprised you have any friends at all."

When I said that, Sora's energy changed dramatically. The confident way she had been holding her body transformed into an awkwardness I had never seen in her before. She slumped over, and her face took on a distant, sad expression.

I stopped talking for a moment to give her some space for the feelings she seemed to be having.

"I've actually been having some trouble with friends recently. But I never thought it might have anything to do with my sportsmanship," Sora said in a softer voice.

"What's been happening with your friends, Sora?" I asked in a way that conveyed to her that I could see that she was having feelings and that I was interested in what she had to say.

"Well, it's mainly been at recess. You know how we usually play basketball or baseball or something like that? Lately, I keep getting picked last or told there's no room left for another player. And I'm good at those games. I had thought that the other kids were just jealous because I'm such a good player, but now I'm wondering ..."

Sora stopped in the middle of her sentence and stared off into space. I didn't say anything and just let there be some space in the conversation. Sometimes a little space allows the person talking time to think about what they want to say. And this seemed like a good time for Sora to think a little more.

"You know," she finally said, "it's not been just at recess. It seems that my friends have been distant and even avoiding me lately. When we're talking, they seem to find excuses for why they have to go, and when I try to make plans with them for the weekend, they say they are busy. It's not all my friends, but a lot of them seem to be that way lately."

"I would bet it's the friends you play sports with who are acting more like that," I probed.

"You're right, Johnny. All my friends from the team seem to be avoiding me."

"After seeing you at practice today, it doesn't surprise me that they would avoid you. You weren't being the best friend to them. Good friends are good team players with each other. And good friends have good sportsmanship with each other.

"If you're not a good sport or good team player with friends, they are not going to trust you or like you. And I have no doubt, Sora, that your poor sportsmanship and trouble being a team player is a big part of why Coach Ity is not playing you in the game on Monday."

"I don't want my friends to hate me," Sora said. "I don't want to be the team bench warmer either. So is there a way I can fix it?"

"That's a great question, Sora. It's the kind of question that shows you are looking to yourself for solutions, rather than just blaming others for your problems. But before we talk about what you can do, there is one more part of sportsman-ship that I think we need to talk about. It has to do with being a gracious loser. A good sport is not only a gracious winner; she is a gracious loser as well.

"During the game, I didn't see anything to suggest that you're not a gracious winner. You never rubbed it in the other team's face when you made an out or scored a run. But when you or someone on your team got out, or when the other team made a good play, you acted, well ... the word that describes it best is 'childish.' You kinda had little temper tantrums any time some-thing didn't go your way. And I would say that having temper tantrums is not a good quality for an athlete who wants to be taken seriously. It's not a good quality for a friend either."

"I don't have temper tantrums!" Sora declared in an indignant voice.

"Would you like a few examples?" I asked.

Sora's face went from indignant to anxious. "Uh, okay, I guess," she said timidly.

"Let's start from the beginning of practice when Coach Ity told you that you were playing right field. Do you remember how you responded?" I asked.

Sora shrugged her shoulders.

"You made a huffy sound and then threw your arms over your head in exasperation. It was clear to everyone, including Coach Ity, that you were … having a tantrum because you had to play right field."

"I couldn't understand why he was playing me in right field," Sora said.

"I can understand you were frustrated about that, but wouldn't you say that huffing off and throwing your hands up in the air in exasperation is, you know, a little childish?"

"I guess you could see it that way," Sora admitted.

"I think Coach Ity definitely saw it that way, because he shook his head disapprovingly when you did it."

"He did?" Sora asked.

"Yup. And I imagine the other kids noticed your reaction and Coach Ity's reaction to you as well. You also grumbled a lot when the players on the other team got on base or made a good play, and when Kyle hit his home run, you groaned so loudly that everyone could hear you. You made so many negative comments that Stewart had to turn around and tell you to shut up. You even talked back to the umpire when you thought he made a bad call. All those things are signs of bad sportsmanship.

"Good athletes have good sportsmanship, which means that they think about the bigger picture. They are not just thinking about how skilled they are at the basics of the game. They are thinking about the bigger picture of the team they are a part of. They are thinking not just about how they can play well, but about how the whole team can play well together.

"And playing well as a team involves a lot more than mastering the basic skills of the game. It involves good team morale. It involves cooperation and good feelings between the players. It involves not being so hard on yourself or on others when mistakes are made. And it involves playing the best you can while not being so attached to winning.

"Winning and losing is the smaller picture. If we get stuck in the smaller picture, all we see is whether or not we win or lose. But the bigger picture, the bigger goal is being the best athlete we can be. Not the best athlete in the world. Not better than someone else. It's about being the best that we personally can be at this particular moment in time. And that involves more than mastering the basic skills. When we are focused on the bigger picture, then we can see that even the losses and errors we make as things that can help us in attaining the bigger goal of becoming a better athlete. And that is how a good sport looks at things."

Sora's eyes were on me the whole time I spoke. Her eye contact and body language made it clear to me that she was paying close attention to what I had been saying.

When I finished talking, Sora shifted her gaze to the distant horizon where the sun was now setting. She gazed thoughtfully towards the oranges and reds that filled the early evening sky.

I joined her, turning my gaze to the glowing colors of the setting sun. I've always loved sunsets. They have a way of making you feel alive and full inside. And they always inspire me to really think about things.

Sora seemed inspired by the sunset as well. After a while she broke the thoughtful silence.

"You know, Johnny, I don't think I ever really thought about the bigger picture before. I mean, you always hear people like your parents talk about how it's not if you win or lose that matter but how you play the game. But come on. Whoever really believes that when mom or dad tell you it? It's always seemed like the kind of thing losers would say to make themselves feel better. But when you think about it, the bigger picture thing does make sense.

"It especially makes sense when you have experienced first-hand, like I have, the negative consequences of poor sportsmanship. But do you know what the worst part of missing the bigger picture is?"

"No, what's the worst part?" I asked.

"The worst part isn't that your friends don't want to play with you. It's not that the coach tells you he isn't going to play you in the most important games of the year. The worst part is that it's painful to feel that you're not good enough if you don't win. It's hard to feel that way all the time. It takes the fun out of the game."

"That makes a lot of sense, Sora. And I bet you are as hard on yourself as you are on your teammates."

Sora stared off towards the setting sun, but this time she talked while looking away. "It's not something I think about really. Being hard on myself just happens. I don't plan to do it. I definitely don't want to do it. Most of the time I don't even realize that I'm doing it. But it happens pretty much every time I play sports. I am way harder on myself than I am on others."

Sora paused again, still looking out towards the sunset.

"It's a strange thing that happens," I continued. "For some reason, the way we are towards others often reflects the way we are towards ourselves. It's not just you this happens to. It happens to us all. Frequently, people who are mean or judgmental towards others are also mean and judgmental towards themselves. Or they expect that others will be just as mean and judgmental to them as they are to everyone else.

"The way we feel about and treat others affects the way we feel about and treat ourselves. And the way we feel about and treat ourselves affects the way we feel about and treat others too. But the good news is that often, when we change the way we are towards others, the way we act towards and feel about ourselves also changes. By becoming more accepting and kind towards other people, we often naturally start being more kind and accepting towards ourselves.

"I would say that if you want to change the way your friends and Coach Ity feel about you, as well as the way you feel about yourself, the best place to start would be with the way you are with others."

Sora brought her eyes back to mine. "I'm not sure I can do that, Johnny. I've always been like this when it comes to sports. It's the same way my dad is, and I imagine his dad was like that, too. And some day my kids will probably be like that. I'm hard on myself, and I'm hard on other people. It just happens."

"Things 'just happen' when you are not thinking about them," I said. "Once you start thinking about them, you become more aware of them. And once you start to become more aware of something, you have some choice as to whether or not it happens. It doesn't 'just happen' any more.

"So let's start with the being hard on yourself part. One of the things you can do to be less hard on yourself is to say more positive things to yourself. I imagine that when you are playing sports, you say a lot of negative, critical things to yourself when your game is not flawless."

Sora nodded her head in agreement.

"You can start to counteract some of the effects of those negative thoughts by responding to them with positive thoughts. You can tell yourself things like 'I'm still a great person even if I make some mistakes,' or 'I don't have to be perfect or the best.' You can remind yourself that it's just a game and that winning isn't everything. And when you make an error or start getting down on yourself, you can tell yourself in a friendly voice, 'It's not a big deal. I'm just going to try my best and enjoy the game.' Things like that will help you to remember the bigger picture, and thinking about that bigger picture will help a lot when it comes to being less hard on yourself.

"Another thing I think would help your attitude towards yourself, as well as towards others, is to keep in mind what I call the Zen of Athletics. The Zen of Athletics consists of the two rules that most of the great, legendary athletes play by. The first rule is to play the best you can all the time. That means you are focused and determined to do your personal best in practice as well as during games, and to always give 110 percent.

"The second rule is the one that people often forget, but it is as important as the first. The second rule is to let go of the outcome. 'Letting go of the outcome' means we are not overly invested in winning or losing. A superior athlete is in it for the game and the sport of it, not for the glory of it. Great athletes strive to do their personal best and give 110 percent while not being overly concerned with whether or not they win.

"The most effective way to do your best is to focus all your attention on what you are doing in this very moment. Our focus and attention help us to perform better. But when we are focused on winning or on other people's performance, our attention is not on ourselves in the present moment. Our attention moves out of the present and into the future when we are focused on winning or losing. And our attention moves away from ourselves when we are over focused on other people's performance. The great athletes are fully present and practicing the Zen of Athletics when they play, and that is a huge part of what makes them great."

I looked to Sora to read her body language. I was saying a lot of things, and I wanted to make sure she was with me. I could tell that she was paying close attention, her eyes fixed on me, her body leaning slightly forward in my direction, with a serious, attentive look on her face. Her facial expression was one of concentration and understanding as opposed to one of confusion, so I continued.

"I think that if you work on those things in yourself, Sora, it will make it much easier to change the way you act with your teammates."

"I can see how the things you suggested could help me be easier on myself, and I really like the Zen of Athletics thing. I will think about that more when I'm playing. But I don't see how that is going to change the way the other kids feel about me," Sora said.

"I imagine that once you start being more positive with yourself and start focusing more on your game, and not as much on how your teammates are playing, you'll start acting differently towards the other kids. And acting differently is probably going to affect how they feel about you quite a bit.

"But it might be helpful to talk about some specific things you can do to change how you interact with your teammates. The first thing you can do is trying to focus more on their strengths, rather than always pointing out their weaknesses. During practice today, you pointed out a lot of weaknesses in your teammates, but I never once heard you say anything positive.

"You never said 'great catch,' 'good hit,' 'nice try,' or anything like that. I would say that for right now, you should only talk about the positives with your teammates so you can try to heal the damage that has been done in your relationship with them."

"But I want my teammates to play their best too, and if I don't say anything it doesn't feel like I'm really helping them," Sora responded in a very serious voice.

"There are many different ways of helping someone, Sora. And one very important way you can help your teammates is by boosting their confidence. When you point out the positive in what others are doing, it not only increases the chances that they will do that positive thing again, it also makes them feel more confident about their abilities in general.

"And confidence in your abilities helps you to play better. Of course, pointing out the positive will help to build better relationships with your friends as well. But when we are critical and focus on the negative, it not only creates a negative relationship with others, it also damages others' sense of confidence in their abilities. And it creates a sense of pressure in them, which keeps them from playing as well as they can. No one plays well when they feel that they are under too much pressure to perform. Remember, the best athletes are not focused on their outcome. They are focused on the present moment and on doing the best they can in that present moment."

"So I should never point out anything negative to my teammates?" Sora asked.

"I would say that at first you should only point out the positive and not say anything at all negative. But once you have healed your relationships with your fellow teammates, there may come a time and place for constructive criticism. It is important to be clear about the difference between constructive criticism and destructive criticism. Constructive criticism is not mean or said to put someone down. It is said in a coaching, supportive way to help someone do better. And constructive criticism usually comes with a helpful, supportive, practical suggestion of what the person could do better.

"Destructive criticism, on the other hand, is said in a mean and often shaming way. While constructive criticism focuses on the positive and on positive change, destructive criticism just focuses on the negative.

"Today at practice, you gave a lot of destructive criticism and no real constructive criticism. For example, when you said to Nick, 'Come on, Nick, get it together,' it was in a mean, angry voice, and you offered nothing positive or helpful."

"I couldn't help it, Johnny. I was irritated, and I wanted him to play better."

"At the time you might not have been able to help it, but now that you are aware of things a little more, I think you will be more capable of helping it in the future. If you really wanted Nick to play better, you could have said something more positive and constructive. You could have said, 'Nice try, Nick; just take your time and focus on the strike zone.'

"Saying something like that would not only have boosted Nick's confidence, which would help him play better, it would also have offered him concrete, constructive suggestions for what he could do to play better. But I encourage you to focus more on being a supportive teammate and just saying things like 'nice try,' rather than on trying to coach the other players. Coaching is Mr. Ity's job, not yours."

At the mention of Coach Ity, Sora's body language went from very still and attentive to twitchy and agitated. She slumped over and moved her body in jerky motions, wrinkling her face in an expression that communicated nothing other than pain.

"Ity's job is to make my life miserable," she bellowed.

"Okay, so let's talk about our dear friend and beloved coach, Arthur Ity," I said with a twist of irony. "Now after everything we have been talking about, do you have a better idea about why Coach might be acting the way he is towards you?" I asked.

Sora's face softened, and her body relaxed and stopped jerking around the way it had been. She looked up at me with big, sad eyes.

"Yeah," she sighed. "I can see why he's not playing me," she said, sighing again. I just wish I had figured it out before I blew my chance of playing in the most important games of the season."

Sometimes as a social detective there is a fine line between the personal and the professional. As a detective, it is important not to get too involved in your client's problems. If you do, you can lose your objectivity and not be able to help solve mysteries well. But the kids I help are usually kids I know, and sometimes they are even friends of mine.

That can make it really hard not getting at least a little personally involved. It is a tricky balance on a good day. But today the balance was way off. I was, I have to admit, very personally involved, not because I was great friends with Sora, but because I really, really … REALLY wanted our team to go to the championships, and I knew that Sora could help that dream come true.

"Okay then," I said with great determination in my voice. "Let's talk about how to deal with Mr. Ity. I think there might still be a chance to get you back in the game. The first thing you need to do, and I recommend you do this tomorrow morning before school starts, is to go to Mr. Ity's office and talk to him. You need to ask him why he is not playing you in the game on Monday and why he is playing you in right field. Make sure you ask him in a very nice way."

"Remember, I told you that I already asked him, Johnny, and he said that if I didn't know by now there was no point in discussing it."

"It's important in situations like that to be persistent," I explained. "If he says the same again tomorrow, tell him that you really want to understand what the problem is so you can make it better. Saying something like that lets people know that you are open to hearing what they have to say. I would also tell him that you think you already know what the problem might be. I would tell him that you realize you have not demonstrated the best sportsmanship lately. Tell him exactly what you see your problem is and give lots of details and examples."

"But won't that just make things worse, Johnny? Isn't that just admitting I'm wrong? Then he really won't want me to play."

"No. It's just the opposite, Sora. When you acknowledge your error, people realize that you understand what your mistake was. And when you can understand what mistake you made, there is a good chance that you won't do the same thing again. But when you don't admit that you made a mistake, people usually just assume that you don't understand what you did wrong.

"And if you don't understand what you did wrong, there is a good chance you are going to do the same thing again. Some people seem to think that if they don't admit to what they did wrong, they will convince the other person that they were right and that that will make things better. But it is almost always the opposite. Not admitting when you are wrong almost always makes things worse, because the other person still knows you did something wrong. But now, because you did not admit to it, the other person thinks that you are not clever enough to understand and learn from your mistakes.

"Give it a try with Coach Ity and see how he responds. I also recommend that you let him know that you understand why he decided not to play you. Another thing kids often try to do is to convince their parents or someone else in a position of authority that they don't deserve the consequences. But here again, this usually just makes things worse.

"By trying to argue why you don't deserve the consequences, you end up giving the message that you don't fully understand what you did wrong and why your actions deserve consequences. All this type of reaction does with parents and authority figures is make them feel an even stronger need to teach you a lesson by giving you consequences.

"But when you really take responsibility and accept the consequences and acknowledge that you deserve them, it sends the message that you learned your lesson. That doesn't mean that you will be let off the hook for what you did. But there is more of a chance that the person doling out the consequences won't feel such a strong need to enforce the consequences to the fullest extent possible because he will think that you understand what you did wrong."

"So you are saying that I should just tell Mr. Ity all the things I did wrong, and tell him I deserve not to play, and then just leave it at that?" Sora asked.

"Exactly," I answered.

"How is that going to help me play in the game, Johnny?"

"Once you have acknowledged what you have done and have taken full responsibility for your actions, by accepting that the consequences are reasonable, then, *and only then*, can you ask if there is anything you can do to rebuild trust. Acknowledging what you did wrong and accepting the consequences is the first, very important step in rebuilding trust.

"But Mr. Ity will probably want to make sure you are not just telling him what he wants to hear. He will probably want to make sure that your actions match your words. I imagine that he will say that he needs to see you behaving differently before he changes his mind. Let him know that you are going to really try to show him how you have changed in practice over the next few days, and that you hope he might reconsider things and let you play in the playoffs.

"And then tell him, and this is important, that you will understand if he still does not want you to play. I'm sure Mr. Ity realizes how much of an asset you can be to the team, if you are being a good team player, Sora. You need to demonstrate to him that you can be a good athlete in all the ways that make someone a valuable member of a team."

The sun had completely disappeared behind the hills by now, and the last rays of light were casting rich shades of orange and pink in the sky. Sora's body language had regained the cool sense of confidence that was so characteristic of her.

"You can be kinda rough, Johnny," Sora said with a playful smile.

"And you can handle it," I shot back in a friendly tone.

We both laughed and gave each other one of those half-nods with a half-smile.

"I'm just trying to talk to you like a good coach would, Sora."

"Thanks for the coaching, Johnny. I'm going to try the things you suggested."

"I hope it works, Sora. I'll be rooting for you. The team needs you."

"The team needs me, and I really need the team, too," Sora said, with a thoughtful look on her face.

 "That is why you want to be the best team player you can be. Because you all need each other to really work. I think this case is officially cracked," I announced.

"Thanks for the help, Coach Multony," Sora said as she slipped off the table and slung her gym bag over her shoulder.

We both laughed.

"Any time, Sora," I said as she walked off.

I really was rooting for her. I was rooting for her professionally like I do with all my social detective clients. And I was rooting for her as a fellow Chipmunk who wanted to show those Hawks just how much damage a little group of Chipmunks could do when they worked together as a team.

Chapter 9

My Way or the Highway: The Case of the Boy Who Couldn't Handle the Gray in Life

His name was Righteous Preachly, and he was, as far as I could tell, a model student. He was an active member of student government, a star on the school debate team and our school finalist for the National School Spirit Speech Contest.

Righteous was a tall boy, with pale skin and short brown hair that always seemed to be perfectly combed. Even though there was not a dress code at our school (thank God!), Righteous almost always wore formal button-down shirts that were neatly tucked into his wrinkle-free pants.

"What can I do for you, Righteous?" I asked in response to his request for a moment of my time in the hallway after English class today.

215

"I would like to inquire about your detective services, Johnny," he said in a very formal tone.

"Sure thing," I said in a voice that was very friendly and informal.

Sometimes people speak in a more formal tone of voice because they are feeling nervous or awkward. When that seems like it might be happening, I try to act extra friendly as a way of helping the other person feel more comfortable.

Righteous and I did not know each other that well, but I had always respected him as a kid who seemed kind of brainy like me.

"I'm on a rather tight schedule right now," he said, "and I don't want to be late for class, but it would be wonderful if I could set up an appointment with you during lunch and discuss the possibility of my enlisting your services."

"Sure, Righteous. Let's meet at lunch then."

"Lunch it is, Johnny. I will meet you at the table in the cafeteria where you usually sit," Righteous said as he reached out to shake my hand.

I extended my hand to meet his, and after a firm shake, we parted ways. Intrigue filled me as it always did when a new case presented itself. But this time I didn't have a clue about what the mystery might be. There was a mystery about the mystery. The suspense would have gotten the best of me if Stan hadn't come along and distracted me.

"So, Johnny. You're coming to my party, right?"

"Are you kidding, Stan? I wouldn't miss it for the world. Your end-of-the-year parties are legendary. The party you threw last year was probably the best party I have been to in my entire life. Kids are still talking about it. And there is a rumor going around. But I can't believe it's true."

"Oh yeah, what rumor is that?" Stan said with a wickedly mischievous grin on his face.

"The rumor is that the Cheese Monkeys will be playing at your party. But that would be insane. There is no way you could get them to play at your party."

Stan, a.k.a. The Dupster, just stared at me with a wild glint in his eyes that said it all.

My voice must have jumped 20 decibels. "No way!" I yelled.

People walking by turned to look. Stan put his finger over his lips in the shhhhh gesture. "I'm trying to keep it at least a little low profile. Even though our backyard is big and my parents said I could invite as many people as I wanted, I don't want the whole city crashing the party."

"How on earth did you get the Cheese Monkeys to play your party, Stan?" I said trying to speak as quietly as my excitement would allow.

"My uncle has been friends with the singer since they were kids. They were in a band together in high school. The Cheese Monkeys are playing at the Megadome the day after my party, and my uncle talked them into coming over and playing at my party. My uncle and some of his old high school buddies will be at the party, and after the Cheese Monkeys play, they are going to hang around and catch up with their old high school friends. And, of course, that means that they will be hanging out with us, too.

"We are going to be partying …" Stan declared in a slightly loud and excited voice, and then caught himself, looking around to make sure no one was listening.

Then again, in a softer voice, "We are going to be partying with the Cheese Monkeys."

"Stan, you are a Party God. I'm feeling the urge to bow down before your God-like feet," I said with a big smile on my face.

Stan lifted his head, pointing his nose in the air and raising his eyebrows in an effort to make the snobbiest face he could, and said, "Yes, you may bow down before me, mortal, and let thy self bask in my God-like party-king presence."

Then, in his usual Dupster style, he asked, "So does that mean you are coming to the party?"

"You had me at 'party,' bro. The Cheese Monkeys just add the thickest, sweetest icing to an already awesome cake. Sign me up, and let me know if you need any help setting up before the party."

"Will do, Johnny," Stan said as the "you better get moving or you're gonna be late for your next class" bell rang.

The thought of seeing the Cheese Monkeys live in Stan's backyard, and actually getting to hang out with them, washed all thoughts of detective work right out of my mind. It wasn't until lunch when I walked over to my usual table and saw Righteous sitting there that I remembered there was a mystery to be solved. Or at least there might be a mystery. There would be no way of knowing for sure until I talked with Righteous.

Tuesday, 12:03 PM

As I approached the table, I saw Righteous looking at his watch and tapping his finger on the table in a way that made it look like he was in a big hurry for something.

"Ah, Johnny there you are," he said as he caught sight of me approaching. "I was beginning to think you'd forgotten about our meeting."

"Why would you think that?" I asked. Actually, I had forgotten, but I could not imagine how he would know that.

"Oh, well, we planned on meeting here at lunch, and lunch is at noon, and, you know, it's after noon now, so I thought you might have forgotten or something."

"I was just getting my lunch," I said as I sat down across from him at the table.

"So tell me what's on your mind, Righteous."

"Well," he said, pausing for a moment to gather his thoughts. "You see, Stan Dupferself is apparently having his big end-of-the-year party in a few weeks. Everyone seems to be invited. I went last year, and the whole school seemed to be there."

"Yeah, Stan's parents are so cool for allowing him to invite so many people to their house. And his parties are definitely legendary," I said, feeling a twinge of Cheese Monkey excitement swim around in my belly as I thought about the party.

"The thing is, everyone seems to be invited to the party. Everyone except me, Johnny," Righteous said.

"Really? It's probably just an oversight, Righteous. You were there last year, right?"

"Yes, I was there last year. But I didn't get an invitation this year. And I don't get the feeling it's an oversight. I don't think Stan wants me to go. In fact, I don't think anyone really wants me to go."

"What makes you think that?" I asked.

"Stan and I used to get along pretty well. Do you know the game called *World of Warcraft*? It's this really cool role-playing game you play on the Internet."

"Yeah, I know the game," I said. I didn't just know the game. I had been a level 70 zombie and was seriously addicted to it a few years back.

"Well," Righteous continued, "you know how you can form clans with your friends and then you all do battles together?"

"Yeah, sure," I said.

"Well, Stan and I, as well as a whole bunch of other kids from school, got together as a team and formed our own clan in the game. We would meet online after school and on the weekends and plan out missions and fight battles together. It was really fun. But for some reason, the team disbanded a few months ago.

"I didn't think much of it at the time. I just assumed that everyone got too busy with other things. But then I found out that all the guys from the old group had formed a new clan, and they didn't include me. At school all those guys seem to avoid me now. And also, when I'm interacting with them, they seem to get irritated with me for no reason."

"Did you do something to make them irritated with you?" I asked.

"I didn't do anything, Johnny. I just don't get it. I always try to be a good, honest friend. I don't understand."

Righteous pulled out his comb and nervously moved it through his hair. Then he fiddled with the collar of his shirt, clasped his hands in front of him and placed his chin on his hands, looking at me expectantly.

"So what do you think, Johnny? Is this something that fits into the line of work you do?"

"It definitely sounds like a mystery to me, Righteous."

"Well then," he said. "I would like to hire you. How do I go about enlisting your services? Is there a contract I need to sign or do you have a description of what you will be doing?"

"No, there's nothing formal like that, Righteous. Basically, I charge a dollar a day plus expenses. And in your particular case, I think I would like to talk to Stan and some of the other guys about why they didn't include you in their new *World of Warcraft* group and about the party, if that's okay with you."

The Case of the Boy Who Couldn't Handle the Gray in Life

"That all sounds fine with me, Johnny. I would really like to figure out what is going on. It is quite unsettling for me." Righteous pulled out a pen and notebook, scribbled down something on a piece of paper, tore it out of the notebook and handed it to me.

There, in meticulously neat handwriting read: "I Righteous Preachly the Third hereby give Jonathan Multony unlimited permission to speak to whomever he sees fit regarding the social mystery he is assisting me in solving." The note was signed and dated.

"Uh, thanks for the note, Righteous."

The note was actually a good idea. I was impressed and, for some reason, a little disturbed by Righteous' formal approach to things.

Righteous proceeded to pull out his wallet and remove a crisp, neatly creased one-dollar bill.

"Here you are, Johnny," he said.

"Thanks, Righteous. Would you like a receipt for that?" I asked jokingly.

"That would be great," he said, not realizing I wasn't serious.

"I was just joking, Righteous. How about a handshake instead?"

"Of course, of course," Righteous said, mustering up a little chuckle and reaching out his hand to give me a firm handshake.

"So what exactly will you be doing, Johnny? Can you give me some details about your approach?"

"I don't like to talk too much about what I will be doing before I do it, because sometimes that can make people act differently than they usually do. So just go about your day as you normally would, and I will take care of the rest."

"Alright then, Johnny. I'll leave it in your hands. Thank you for your help." Righteous stood up and extended his hand to offer a parting handshake, then left me to finish my lunch.

Righteous was an interesting kid. While he was someone I had noticed for his school achievements on many occasions, he was not someone who I gave much thought to in terms of his social achievements.

One of the great things about being a social detective is that you get to know people in very personal ways, which you might never have had an opportunity to experience if you were not a social detective. It's one of the many reasons I love my job.

Wednesday, Beginning of Third Period

I decided to start my investigation off with a stake-out and observation of Righteous in action. It's often helpful to see first-hand how a client is with other people, before doing other things like interviewing eyewitnesses. Or, in this case, interviewing ex-friends like those who were in Righteous' old *World of Warcraft* clan.

Third period on Wednesdays is electives. My elective this semester is an independent project on how computer technology might affect society in the future. That's how you say, in a way that is acceptable to teachers, that you are going to research and write a paper about how amazing computer games might be in the future.

And the best part of that independent project is that I get to spend most of my elective class time in the library surfing the Internet to find out what computer game companies are planning. Sure, I'll be talking about some computer technology other than games, but computer gaming will be the main theme.

But today I wouldn't be surfing the net. Today I'd be using my elective time to get a glimpse of Righteous in action. His elective is debate team, and they always met in the auditorium. The auditorium stage was flooded with spotlights, which made it easy for me to slip in the back and take a seat in a shadowy corner.

When I arrived, Rory and Elisa were each standing at podiums facing the audience. The rest of the class was in the first few rows. I was sitting far behind the kids in the class, and the bright lights shining on the stage meant all I could make out was the shadowy silhouettes of everyone's heads. It was impossible from that angle to make out which head might be Righteous'. So I waited patiently, observing the scene and keeping my eyes and ears open for clues.

Rory and Elisa were debating a law proposing to raise the legal age for driving from 16 to 18. Rory was arguing that kids should be allowed to drive when they are 16, and Elisa was arguing that kids should wait until they are 18.

Eventually, Rory and Elisa finished their debate, and the class gave them feedback on how they did. Next up were Avi and Righteous. Their topic was whether it would be right or wrong for someone who had no money and no other way of getting the medicine to steal medicine from a drugstore to save their sick child's life.

Avi began the debate. "I believe that if someone had no money and no other way of getting the medicine, stealing it would be the right thing to do," he said very confidently.

He continued, "Not only would it be the right thing to do, but not stealing the medicine would be morally wrong. If you didn't steal the medicine, your child could die, and that is a much worse offense than stealing."

Righteous responded, saying, "I disagree with you. I believe that it would be very wrong to steal, no matter what. There is no excuse for stealing. Rules are made to protect people, and we need to follow the rules that society has set up for us. If we didn't, then that would be immoral."

Righteous was very passionate about what he said. You could tell by the tone of his voice that he really believed what he was saying and that he felt very strongly about it.

"But sometimes the rules don't apply to every situation," Avi said in response. "In fact, rules that have the good intention of protecting people can, in a certain situation, actually cause harm to someone. I agree that not stealing is a very good rule in general. And I agree that it serves to help protect people. But it is important to look at the bigger picture when deciding whether a rule is good or not.

"The rule of not stealing is usually a great rule. But in this situation, following that rule does not protect the child who needs the medicine. In fact, the rule hurts the child. So, while in many situations the rule of not stealing is good, in this situation it is not."

Righteous looked irritated, and his voice went from passionate to a little angry. "So you're saying that we can just decide when rules should be followed and when they should not be followed? That would lead to chaos in a society, and everybody would start doing whatever he or she felt like. You could say that if I don't steal this candy bar, I will not be happy, so I'll just steal it because I've decided that in this situation the rule not to steal does not benefit me. And what about the store owner? If you steal the medicine, then the storeowner is not being protected. He is out of the money he paid for the medicine. Does that seem right?"

Righteous was clearly getting worked up. Avi, on the other hand, was keeping his cool. "Well," Avi responded. "The point I'm making is that you need to figure out what's most important in any situation. Is following the rules more important than the child's health? I would say no. Is the store owner losing a little money more important than the child's health? Again, I would say no. But I would also say that fulfilling your desire to eat a candy bar is less important than following rules and less important than the store owner losing money, so in that situation stealing would be wrong."

"You just don't seem to get it," Righteous protested. "Rules are meant to be followed. You can't just pick and choose when to follow them to suit what you think is right and wrong. That would lead to total chaos. And not only that, you would get into trouble.

"Do you think that the police are going to say, 'Oh, well, you stole the medicine for your sick child, so I guess it's okay then'? No. They're not going to care what you think is right. They are going to follow the rules because that is what moral people do. Good, honest, moral people follow the rules, and that is that," he concluded with great confidence in his voice.

The buzzer went off indicating that they had used up their allotted debating time. The class gave them feedback and then moved onto the next debate team. Righteous and Avi blended back into the sea of silhouettes sitting in front of me. I didn't think I would get much more from watching the rest of the class, so I decided I would pick up my surveillance again at lunchtime.

Wednesday, 11:58 AM

I spotted Righteous walking towards the cafeteria with the other students from the debate team, so I slotted myself strategically behind them in the herd of kids.

As I was inconspicuously tailing them, I overheard Righteous talking to Avi. "So you don't really think it's okay to steal, do you?" he said with a definite tone of judgment in his voice.

"It's important to take the bigger picture into account," Avi replied.

"That's just stupid. No one in their right mind would think such a thing."

"Well," Avi said, still keeping his cool, "there are actually many people who think that. In fact, many people believe that being able to think about the needs of the child in this situation, and not just think about the rules, is a sign of maturity. They believe that mature people are better able to be flexible with rules and understand that a rule may be valid in one situation but not in another situation."

"Well, I think anyone who would say that is not very intelligent. It's just not logical. It's … it's not right. You are either right or wrong about something. To say that it is right to steal in one situation and wrong in another is just not logical. Anyone who would say that is not smart enough to realize that they are contradicting themselves."

Righteous's tone was critical, and Avi's response was simple and clear.

"Whatever, Righteous," Avi finally said, and turned his attention to Rory and Steven, who were excitedly talking about the Cheese Monkeys.

I wasn't sure if they knew yet that they were playing at Stan's party, but they did know that their new album was out and that they were playing at the Megadome in a few weeks.

"The new album is awesome!" Steven said enthusiastically, as the group of kids sat down to eat their lunch.

I took a seat at the table just behind the group. It was a great surveillance spot. I was facing the group, and Righteous' back was to me so he couldn't see me. It was close enough so that I was able to hear every word they were saying and even see the facial expressions of many of the kids.

But as far as anyone else knew, I was just another kid having my lunch. I pulled out all the lunchtime goodies my mom had packed and began eating, so as to not bring any suspicion to my being there.

"'Swingin' from the Trees' is one of the coolest songs I've ever heard!" Rory added. "It is totally original!"

Righteous snickered at Rory's comment.

"What?" Rory turned to Righteous, surprised at his reaction.

"Original? I'd hardly use that word to describe it."

"Have you even heard it?" Steven asked in a defensive tone of voice.

"I got the album the day it came out," Righteous replied. "I loved their last album. It had all the elements of the perfect album. The songs were perfectly written. Great verses. Catchy choruses. The songs were not too long and not too short. Perfect.

"But this album is terrible. What were they thinking?" Righteous sneered. "It is totally different from their last album. It sounds like a different band. I wouldn't even call 'Swingin' from the Trees' a song. Songs have a beginning, a middle and an end. The whole thing is just one catchy riff with lots of sound effects playing over it. And it's seven minutes long. That is way longer than a song should be. It's like they lost all their musical abilities and forgot how to write a pop song."

"It's called being original and experimental, Righteous," Steven said. "And the music critics seem to love it, because they are giving the album incredible reviews. They are saying it is brilliant, fresh, innovative, and ..."

Steven paused, clearing his throat, straightening his posture and making his facial expression look very formal and proper, in an effort to give the impression that he was the music critic announcing his opinion of the album ... *"incredibly original."*

"Those critics don't know what they are talking about. There is a way good music is written, and the Cheese Monkeys seem to have totally forgotten how to do that," Righteous repeated.

"Well, that's your opinion, Righteous," Avi added.

"No, it's not my *opinion*. It's the truth. Someone might think it's good music if they don't have a real understanding of what good music is. But the Cheese Monkeys have totally lost their groove if you ask me."

"Well, I'll be sure not to ask you then," Rory said and chuckled.

The other guys in the group laughed as well, which seemed to break some of the tension.

The conversation moved to a variety of other subjects, all of which Righteous seemed to have very strong opinions about. Soon the lunch bell rang, and the group rose from the table and blended into the crowd of kids.

I had got few some good leads, but I still wanted to question some of the guys from Righteous' old *World of Warcraft* clan.

Wednesday, 3:14 PM

I spotted Stan and Trevor on the field talking, and thought it would be the perfect opportunity to do some good old-fashioned detective questioning.

Trevor was one of the guys in Righteous' old *World of Warcraft* clan. Trevor looked like a cross between a skater and a rocker. He had long, brown hair that even on the calmest of days looked like it was blowing in the wind. And he always had his Oakley sunglasses attached to some part of his body. They would either be covering his eyes, sometimes even when he was inside, or they would be propped on is head, serving as a sort of bandana to keep his hair from getting in his face.

As I approached, Stan was the first to see me. He was standing up facing in my direction, while Trevor was leaning up against a tree.

"What's up, Johnny?" Stan asked, interrupting the flow of his conversation with Trevor to greet me.

"Not much. Whatcha up to?" I replied.

"Hey, Johnny," Trevor said in a friendly voice as he moved from his leaning position on the tree. He offered up his hand in the slightly angled way that is the prompt for the hand-shake, pop, knuckle-bump combo greeting that is so popular these days. Instead of the traditional handshake, you kind of slap palms with each other, making a popping sound as your palms meet. You follow that up by making a fist and gently touching knuckles with the person you are greeting.

"What's happening, Trev?" I asked, while we were doing our handshake, knuckle bump.

"Ahh, you know. Same old stuff. Hanging out, skating, playin' some tunes. We're planning a big battle online and trying to come up with some strategies."

"Yeah, I heard you guys have your own clan. Are you Hoard or Alliance?" I asked.

The truth was that I asked the question not just because I wanted to know. I asked the question to show them that I knew something about *World of Warcraft*. Because only some-one who knew the game would know that the Hoard and the Alliance are the two factions in the game.

"We're Hoard. Do you W.O.W.?" Trevor asked with some ex-citement in his voice.

W.O.W. was the term gamers used for *World of Warcraft*, and 'Do you W.O.W.?' was sort of the secret question that only someone who was a member of this underground society could answer.

The Case of the Boy Who Couldn't Handle the Gray in Life

"Oh yeah," I said. "I used to be a level 70 Zombie."

"Dude!" Trevor said, very excited now. "Level 70! You should totally play with us. We are always looking for cool people to come join the cause."

"Yeah, Johnny," Stan added energetically. "That would be so cool to have you be in our clan!"

"Thanks, you guys. That is a tempting offer. I would totally love to play with you guys, but I have to think about it. I've got so much stuff going on right now that I'm not sure how much time I could really commit to the game. And if I did join, I would want to make sure I could be there for the team."

It was cool that they invited me to join them, and I wanted to be extra clear that any hesitation on my part had nothing to do with them. It had nothing to do with not liking them or wanting to spend time with them. When people invite you to do things with them, they make themselves vulnerable in a sense, and, if people do not feel like you appreciate their invitation, it's easy for them to take it as a rejection, which can affect how they feel about you as a friend.

"Well, think about it, Johnny, 'cauz it would be great to have you," Stan said.

"Thanks, guys. That's very cool of you to offer, and I can't think of anyone I'd rather have as clan members. Let me check my schedule, and I'll let you know," I said.

"Sounds good," Trevor added. The talk about the *World of Warcraft* clan offered the perfect bridge, a perfect transition to my investigation.

"Hey, speaking of your clan, I have a question for you guys. I heard Righteous was in your clan a while back. Did you guys kick him out?"

Stan and Trevor looked at each other. It was one of those looks that seemed to consist of a mix of many different feelings. From my point of view, it looked like a combination of guilt, irritation and mischievousness.

"Johnny, that boy could use your social detective help. He has got some serious issues," Trevor offered.

"Funny you should say that, Trev, 'cauz I am actually working with him right now. Normally, I keep who I'm working for confidential, but Righteous gave me permission to talk to whoever I wanted, if it would help to solve his mystery," I explained.

"What's his mystery?" Stan asked.

I laughed a little and looked at Stan with a big smile on my face to make it clear that there was no judgment or hint of criticism in what I was about to say.

"It is the mystery of why he was not invited to your end-of-the-year party."

Stan's eyes got huge, and his mouth opened. Then he let out a sort of guttural laughing sound. You could tell by the tense quality of Stan's laugh that he thought what I had said was a little funny, a little embarrassing and definitely not what he was he was expecting me to say.

"Probably not the answer you expected, huh?" I said, laughing some myself. My laughing seemed to help break the tension a little.

"I personally have no investment in whether Righteous goes to your party or not, Stan. After all, the fewer people who show up, the better my chances of getting a front-row spot for the Cheese Monkeys," I said, laughing again. "But Righteous is confused about why he was not invited and wants to figure it out."

Trevor started laughing, too. This time, it was one of those closed-mouth laughs. The kind of laugh that you are trying to hold in because somehow it does not seem appropriate, but it just slips out of the corners of your mouth, making a spurting sound as it escapes.

"Sorry," Trevor said, referring to his laughter spurts. "It's just …" He cleared his throat trying, unsuccessfully I might add, to keep himself from laughing again. "It's just, the look on your face, Stan. You look like Johnny just told you that you were accidentally switched at birth and that Mrs. Krabington was your long-lost mother."

We all started laughing at the idea of that scenario. "I can promise you that the look on my face if that were the case would be a look of total, absolute, ultimate horror. And there would be lots of screaming," Stan commented. "This was more of a look of … I don't know; I guess I feel kinda bad for not inviting Righteous. I mean, I invited so many other people. But he has become so irritating I can't handle it. And I'm not the only one who feels that way, am I, Trevor?" Stan asked, turning his gaze in Trevor's direction.

"It's true. The guy has developed this incredible ability to piss people off," Trevor agreed.

"Is that why he is not in your W.O.W. clan any more?"

"Yup," Stan and Trevor said in stereo. Stan continued, "We told him at the time that we were disbanding the clan. We didn't want to hurt his feelings by telling him that the rest of us were sick of him. But I think he must have realized that we didn't want him in our group, because he found out that we had started a new clan and didn't invite him."

"What did he do to irritate you guys so much?" I continued.

"He became so controlling," Stan explained. "He was always telling us that we were not following the rules perfectly. He was constantly quoting the official *World of Warcraft* handbook. He started telling us how we should make decisions in the group and how things were not fair if we didn't agree with him. And when we came up with strategies for the game, he constantly told us that we were not following traditional military protocol. Traditional military protocol! Where did that come from?

"We kept reminding him that this was not the military – that it was just a game. But he kept saying that if we wanted to win and if we wanted to play properly, we had to play the game 'the way it was supposed to be played.'"

"The worst part was that he was rude when we saw things differently. He never said he had a different opinion. I can handle different opinions. He would just tell us we were wrong. Anything that was different from his point of view was wrong. It wasn't different. It was wrong. Frequently, he wouldn't even listen to anyone else's opinion. He would just tell them they were wrong without even knowing what they were going to say.

Do you know how irritating it is to be told you are wrong without even having a chance to explain how you see things?" Stan's voice was getting louder and louder, and more and more irritated as he talked.

Trevor jumped in to continue where Stan left off. "What made things even worse," he went on, "was the way Righteous would talk to us when telling us how wrong we were and how right he was. He would talk down to us like he knew it all and we knew nothing. And he would get nasty and say critical things like we weren't smart enough to understand the truth.

"But the thing that pushed us all to the point where we totally couldn't handle him any more was his relentlessness. He would not stop talking about how wrong we were when we didn't agree with him. It was like he thought that if he kept making his point over and over, he would somehow break us down and get us to agree with him. I cannot tell you how incredibly annoying that can be."

Stan jumped back in. "Finally, we all just had enough. I mean, Righteous is not a bad guy. He has some good qualities, and none of us wanted to hurt his feelings."

"We just wanted some peace," Trevor added.

"Is that also why you didn't invite him to your party?" I asked.

"Yeah, I guess that's part of it," Stan said. "The last few months have been kinda tense with Righteous anyway. It seems like every time I'm around him, he is telling people how they are not doing things the right way, or something like that. He seems to be pissing a lot of people off these days.

"But the clincher that made me cross him off my party list happened a few weeks ago. It was just after the new Cheese Monkeys album came out. He was going around telling everyone how terrible it was. He was relentless and extremely harsh and critical. He was irritating people left and right and just did not know when to quit.

"I heard people tell him to drop it, but he continued ranting until people would just walk away from him while he was talking. The way he was acting seemed totally inappropriate. When I heard him ranting like that, I imagined him at my party telling the Cheese Monkeys how bad he thought their album was, and that if they were really good musicians, they would have written their songs differently. Can you imagine what that would be like?"

"Oh my God, I could totally see Righteous doing that," Trevor said, laughing at the thought of it.

Stan went on, "I couldn't risk the chance of that happening. It would be a catastrophe."

"That would be really messed up," I agreed. "It makes a lot of sense, Stan. You guys expressed that so well, too. A lot of people who had the experience you did with Righteous would probably just sum up their experience by saying that Righteous is a jerk.

"But you guys expressed exactly why he has been a jerk. Is it cool with you guys if I share what you said with Righteous? I think it could help him a lot."

"If you think it will help, it's cool with me," Stan said. "Just make sure to share it in a way that doesn't make it out like we are just bagging on him. Like I said, Righteous isn't a bad guy, and I don't want him to just think we all hate him."

"I will definitely be careful with how I share it with him. But the truth is that sometimes it is better to hear the truth, even if it hurts. Sometimes the truth, if told with good intention and not to hurt, can help people to see what they are doing to make others not like them. And I'd say that in most situations, knowing the truth about what you are doing to irritate people is much better than just going around unaware.

"When you are unaware of what you are doing, you are more likely to just think other people are mean. But when you are aware of what you are doing, even though it might hurt, you have an opportunity to do something different," I said.

"Well, I hope Righteous decides to do something different. And if sharing what we said can help Righteous to stop being so annoying, then you have my blessing," Trevor concluded.

"With your guys' help, I think it is safe to say that this mystery is solved."

 ## Can You Solve the Case of the Boy Who Couldn't Handle the Gray in Life?

Here are some questions that might help you in solving the case:

- How would you describe the mystery?

The Case of the Boy Who Couldn't Handle the Gray in Life

- What are the facts in this case?

- How would you make sense of the facts?

- What are the biggest clues?

- What does Righteous see as the problem?

- What do you think Johnny would see as the problem?

- Why do you think Righteous was kicked off the *World of Warcraft* team and not invited to Stan's party?

- What clues did Johnny find to help him solve the case?

- Was Righteous respectful of other people's opinions?

- How do you think you would feel if Righteous talked to you the way he talked to Avi?

- Why do you think Steven and Rory responded to Righteous the way they did?

- Do you think rules were too important to Righteous or not important enough?

- Do you think you would be friends with Righteous? Why?

- What social remedies would you offer to Righteous?

- How would you test out your social remedies to see if they are working?

Cracking the Case

Wednesday, 5:45 PM

When I arrived home, after a tasty snack, homework and a marathon wrestling match with Thor, my feisty golden retriever, I emailed Righteous to let him know I had solved his case.

He responded immediately. "Thank you for attending to my case in such a timely manner. I am very anxious to hear your findings," he wrote.

Sometimes the way Righteous spoke seemed incredibly formal, and when he wrote it was even more formal.

I wrote back, suggesting we meet Friday during lunch.

"I am very anxious to hear your findings," he replied. "Could you possibly write them up and send me a report this evening?"

"I don't write reports," I wrote back.

"Then could we meet tonight? I would be more than happy to come over to your house. I believe that you live just a few blocks away from me."

"I usually like to have some time to sit with a case before I present it to my client, so tomorrow would be better," I said.

The Case of the Boy Who Couldn't Handle the Gray in Life

Tonight was also the season finale of *Stargate Atlantis*, and there was no way I was going to miss a single precious moment of that.

"How about we meet at lunch tomorrow and go over the findings?" I suggested.

"If part of your procedure is having some time before you share your findings, I certainly do not want to interfere with that. But I always eat lunch with the debate team on Thursdays, and I don't want to interfere with that routine. Can we meet in the morning? How about 7:30 at school by the flag pole?" Righteous countered.

"Okay. I think I can get there by 7:30. I'll see you tomorrow, then," I wrote back.

"Splendid. Then it is a date. 7:30 sharp by the flagpole." He ended his message with "Sincerely, Righteous Preachly."

That was the first time I had ever seen a kid sign off like that. Usually it was something like "Later dude," "Smell you later" or just the simple and to the point, "Bye."

Righteous was a "proper" boy, which, I think, added to some of the problems he was having. But that was enough about Righteous for one day. It was getting close to *Stargate* time.

Thursday, 7:32 AM

I arrived at the flagpole to see Righteous waiting for me, not so patiently.

"You're late," he said, tapping his watch.

I looked at my watch. "It's 7:32," I said.

"Didn't we say 7:30?" Righteous countered.

I was irritated that Righteous was making a big deal about me being two minutes late. I was especially irritated because I had originally wanted to meet later, but had agreed to meet earlier at his request.

"Don't you think you're being a little nit-picky, Righteous?" I asked, trying to contain my irritation so it would not show. After all, I was trying to help him solve his social mystery, and clearly this type of behavior was directly related to his problem.

"I think being on time is important. And I think that when you make an agreement, it is important to keep it," Righteous said.

"Do you always give people a hard time if they are a minute or two late?" I asked.

"Huh ... yeah probably. Wouldn't you?" he asked.

"If someone was really late, I would probably say something. But come on, Righteous. Two minutes? You seemed upset yesterday when I wasn't there at the table at exactly 12 o'clock."

"Okay, okay," I'm sorry. Can we just get on to your findings?" Righteous said impatiently, looking again at his watch.

"I think that what we're talking about right now is related to your case."

"How is your being late related to my case?" he asked, with a look of surprise on his face.

"It's your reaction to my being two minutes late that's important. Let me ask you a question, okay? Do you think that you are a little rigid and inflexible at times?" I asked.

"Why, because I was upset that you were late?" Righteous snapped back.

"You were upset because I was two minutes late. And you seemed bothered yesterday when I was not sitting at the lunch table at exactly 12 o'clock."

"Well, yesterday we said we would meet at the table at lunch and, when you weren't there at 12, I thought you might have forgotten," Righteous explained.

"I don't think we agreed that we would meet at 12 sharp and

not to be a second late. It takes time to get your food, and someone might have to go to the bathroom or something like that."

"Well, then we should have discussed those possibilities. Or maybe I should have been more clear, and requested that we meet at 12:00 o'clock sharp, or 12:05 sharp?"

"Or how about being a little more flexible and saying, 'Hey, I'll meet you there at lunch,' and then just relaxing if the other person isn't there at the exact same moment you are?"

"That's not how I do things, Johnny."

"I realize that, Righteous, and I think that is a big part of your problem."

I sat down on the grass and invited Righteous to join me. "Shall I share with you some of what I observed?" I asked.

"Yes. Please do," Righteous said eagerly as he sat down beside me.

"Let's start at the beginning. I watched your debate with Avi yesterday and ..."

"Really? How did you get in there? I mean, did you get permission to come watch the debate?" Righteous asked.

"Let's just say I was doing some undercover work and managed to get in there without anyone noticing."

"You know you're not supposed to do that, Johnny. You could get in trouble."

"Would you like to talk about the rules, Righteous, or would you like to hear about my findings?"

"Okay, sure. It's just that I don't think it's right to …"

"Shall I continue?" I asked, again trying to contain my irritation so it would not come out and affect my professional way of interacting with Righteous.

"During the debate, you followed the rules very well. You took turns expressing your ideas and responded to what others said. While I have to admit that I didn't agree with your position, the way you expressed it in the context of the debate seemed okay. But after the debate, you did a number of things that I think may help to explain why kids are having some problems with you."

Righteous' eyes were on me, letting me know he was attending closely to what I was saying. His attention was my cue to keep going.

"After class, you continued the conversation with Avi."

"How did you know that?" Righteous asked, a slightly surprised look on his face.

With a smug and slightly mysterious expression, I replied, "I'm a detective. It's my job to know these things."

I continued. "The way you spoke to Avi was not very respectful. You responded to his expressing his opinion by saying things like 'That's just stupid' and 'No one in their right mind would think such a thing.' At one point you even responded to what he was saying with 'I think anyone who would say that is not very intelligent.'

"Basically, what you were saying to Avi was that he was stupid, not very intelligent and not in his right mind for having the opinions he had."

"I know those probably weren't the nicest things to be saying. But he was making me angry. I mean, did you hear what he was saying about stealing?"

"I did hear what he was saying, Righteous, and I want to come back to that in a minute because I think your debate topic holds some important clues that can help us crack your case. But let me share some more of my findings before we get to that."

Righteous nodded, and I continued.

"Your conversation moved onto the new Cheese Monkeys album. The other guys were expressing their enthusiasm for it, but your response to their enthusiasm was to tear the album apart. You criticized the Cheese Monkeys in a way similar to how you criticized Avi, saying that their new album was 'terrible' and that they have 'lost all their musical abilities.'

"You also criticized Rory and Steven and basically anyone who might disagree with your opinion by saying 'someone might think it's good music if they didn't really have an understanding of what good music was.'

"Basically, what you were saying was that the only reason someone might disagree with you would be that they didn't know what good music was. In a sense, you were saying that your opinions are the ultimate truth and that anyone who sees things differently is wrong. Can you understand how that might affect other people, Righteous? Can you understand how that kind of attitude can come across as arrogant and very judgmental?"

"It's the way I see things, Johnny. Sometimes I think people are just wrong about things."

"You're entitled to your opinions, Righteous. But it would be beneficial to your friendships to think about how the way you express things affects others. How would you feel if someone said things to imply that you were stupid and had no understanding of music? I imagine it would bother you and affect how close you felt to that person."

"Yeah, I guess so," Righteous admitted. "But I see people being wrong a lot, and it makes me angry when they can't see things the right way."

"I think part of the problem you are having, Righteous, is that you seem to have difficulty seeing that there may be more than one right way of looking at things. It seems that you think things are either black or white, and that there is nothing in between. It seems that it may be hard for you to understand that there are actually many shades of gray in between the black and the white."

I always look for clues about how someone is reacting to what I am saying. The look on Righteous' face was one of someone who was confused, which was good feedback for me and led me to ask him if what I was saying made sense.

"You lost me with the black-and-white thing, Johnny," Righteous said.

"Let me give an example that might make it clearer. When you talked about the new Cheese Monkeys album, you judged it in terms of being either good or bad, black or white. It seems that it's difficult for you to see that it's not as simple as that. It seems like it is difficult for you to understand that the album might be great for some people and not so great for others. Or that it might be good in some ways and not so good in other ways.

"To you, it is either all good or all bad. That's what I mean by 'black or white.' It is either all one way – all black. Or it is all the other way – all white. But the truth is that most things in life are not all one way or the other. They are not all good or all bad. They're not all black or all white. Many things in life can be looked at in a variety of ways that can lead to seeing them as both good in some ways and bad in others. And the blending of black and white makes gray.

"If you are measuring the value of a piece of music by how well it fits the formula for how you think songs should be written, you could say the Cheese Monkeys album is bad. But if you are measuring the value of a piece of music in terms of how it makes you feel or how creative and different it is, then you could say that, for many people, the new Cheese Monkeys album is excellent. In a situation like this, deciding if something is good or bad all depends on how you look at it. It's not just black and white. It's not that simple."

"I guess that makes sense, Johnny," replied Righteous. "But I like rules, and I like it when they're followed. And sometimes I get confused and stressed when things are not black and white."

"I can understand that, Righteous. Living in a world where things are not always black and white can be confusing. But there are lots of good things that come from all the shades of gray. The most important thing in terms of your case, though, is that the world is not black and white, and it is important to be able to respect when people do not see things the way you do. Maybe you can even learn something from other people's points of view that will open up your world and offer you new and exciting ways of looking at things."

What I was talking about was kind of complicated, so I wanted to make sure I was being clear. I looked for feedback from Righteous again and saw that he was still looking a little confused.

"Does what I'm saying make sense?" I asked.

"It does make some sense," Righteous replied. "But I'm not sure what you mean by saying I can learn something from other people's points of view."

"Okay. Let me give you an example that might make it clearer. Take the new Cheese Monkeys album. What would happen if you just listened to how it made you feel, rather than analyzing it to see if it fit a certain formula for how you think music should be? If you tried to look at it from that different point of view, you might actually find something worthwhile in it."

"That's easier said than done," Righteous argued. "It's hard for me to put the rules aside like that. It makes me nervous. When I think about it, that's how I felt about Avi's argument for stealing in the debate. It might have seemed like I was mad, but I don't think I was mad as much as I was stressed and nervous about what he was saying. I mean, the idea of living in a world where people don't follow the rules seems really overwhelming to me."

"Sure. That makes sense, Righteous. But sometimes there are bigger rules at work that you may not be seeing. There are often the simple rules of right and wrong. Like 'It's wrong to steal, and it's right not to steal.'

"But sometimes different situations have different rules. I'll give you some examples.

"Running is 'right' in some situations like on the playground, but 'wrong' in other situations like in class, right?"

"Yeah, that's true," Righteous agreed.

"Yelling is totally acceptable, and even called for, in some situations, like when you are rooting for your team at a baseball game, but it is totally unacceptable in other situations like at the library."

Righteous nodded his head in agreement.

"So how about calling someone a butthead?" I asked.

Righteous' eyes widened, and he laughed a little. "No, that would never be okay," he said in a very confident voice.

"Really?" I probed. "How about if you are joking around with your buddies, and you all know you are joking and that it's just in fun. Would that be okay?"

Righteous looked a little confused. "I guess if you were joking, and the other person knew you were joking, it might be okay. But if they didn't know you were joking, it would not be okay. And even if they knew you were joking, but they were in a bad mood or talking about something serious, it wouldn't be okay."

"Exactly!" I said. "There are shades of gray there. And when there are shades of gray, things can get complicated. It would be so much simpler if it were just right or wrong to call someone a butthead. There would be so much less to have to think about, and people probably would not get confused about when it's okay and when it's not. But if it were just wrong to call someone a butthead, you would miss out on the fun that comes when it's okay to call your friends that."

"Okay, Johnny, I can see your point there. But how about stealing? I can't ever see it being right to steal. There are no shades of gray there," Righteous protested.

"Well, let's look at that one. Let me ask you this. Would it be right to let someone die if there was something simple you could do to prevent it?"

"That's not a fair question, Johnny. You're twisting the issue of stealing and turning it around so that ..." Righteous trailed off, huffing a little.

At first, the look on his face seemed angry, but then I realized it was not anger it reflected. It was anxiety and confusion.

"It's not that it is an unfair question, Righteous. It's that it is not a simple question. It is not a black-and-white question. It is a question that can be looked at from many different angles that can seem contradictory. When you look at it from the angle of social rules and laws, it seems clear that you should not steal. When you are looking at it simply from that point of view, the answer seems very black and white. The answer would very clearly be 'you should not steal.'

"If you look at it only from the point of view of whether or not you could stop a person from dying, the answer is different, but also very clear. And the answer, for most caring people, would be that, of course, you should do something if it can save someone's life. From this limited perspective, the answer once again is black and white and simple.

"What makes it tricky is when you have to acknowledge both points of view at the same time. Holding both points of view turns what was black and white into something very gray. It turns a simple right-or-wrong situation into a complex situation that can be confusing and make you anxious.

"So how do you deal with the anxiousness and the shades of gray?" I asked.

Righteous shrugged.

"My guess is that the way you deal with anxiety is to pretend that things are simpler than they really are. You see, some people can't see that there are different ways of looking at things. Some people might not be able to see that, while stealing is wrong, not helping someone by getting them medicine is also wrong. They might not be able to see the bigger picture of saving someone's life and might only be able to see the smaller picture of following the rules.

"Little kids are often like this. They are not yet able to understand the bigger picture that includes both the rules about not stealing and the rules about taking care of people. But I can tell by the things you are saying, Righteous, that you are capable of understanding that the bigger picture holds both of those truths."

"When you describe things the way you did, I can definitely see the bigger picture," Righteous said. "But what I can't see is any good solution to the problem. If you steal and save the person's life, you help someone, which is good, but you are still stealing, which is bad. If you don't help the person, you are not stealing, which is good, but you are not helping the person who is sick, which is bad. Either way you end up losing. In this situation, the rules are not really helping to solve the problem, and that makes me anxious," Righteous concluded looking down at his hands and cracking his knuckles nervously.

"And when you are anxious about things like that," I proceeded, "I imagine you just pick one position and try to convince yourself that is the one and only truth. Then you end up saying something like 'Stealing is wrong, and that is that,' and don't pay attention to any information that might contradict that point of view. You convince yourself it's just black and white, and that way you don't have to feel the anxiousness that comes with the uncertainty of not knowing what to do."

"Well, what would you do, Johnny? I mean, if you were to be in a situation like that, where someone was going to die if you didn't steal the medicine for them. How would you deal with it? If you take both points of view into consideration, one part of you would be saying, 'Steal the medicine,' because not helping the sick person would be wrong, and another part would be saying, 'Don't steal it,' because stealing is wrong. The dilemma would end up leaving you paralyzed and confused and probably anxious like me."

Righteous spoke in a tone that, if I didn't know better, I would have interpreted as irritation rather than anxiety.

"It's not that there is no answer in a situation like this. It's just that the answer is not as simple when you look at the bigger picture. In this situation, the bigger picture consists of two smaller pictures or points of view. One of these smaller points of view has to do with the issue of stealing, and the other has to do with the issue of doing something to help save a sick person. The bigger point of view, which I call the bigger picture, takes both of these smaller points of view into consideration.

"To make sense of things from this bigger point of view, you need to find a way to measure what is most important. I think that is kind of what Avi was trying to say in the debate."

"So you agree with Avi?" Righteous probed.

"Yeah. Actually I do, and I'll tell you why. For me the value of a human life is a higher priority than the value of not stealing from a drugstore. Now the value of eating an ice cream is a way lower priority than the value of being honest and not stealing. So I could never justify stealing an ice cream. But in my value system, letting someone die when you could prevent it is a much worse crime than stealing something. It is a worse crime to me because I value human life more than I value money. But I would definitely value someone's right not to be robbed above someone's desire for ice cream."

Righteous looked at me. Then he looked down at his knuckles, cracking them again. But this time the cracking was not as desperate as before. He pushed on each finger and then gently picked at the nail on his right thumb, turning his head slightly from side to side. I could tell he was thinking, so I gave him some space.

Finally, after a fair amount of knuckle cracking and thumb picking, Righteous looked up at me.

"So what do you think about all that?" I asked.

"I think you should join the debate team, because you just tore my argument to shreds. I guess I was wrong and you were right," he said.

"Wrong and right. Black and white. It's probably not as simple as that," I said with a smile.

Righteous laughed. "Okay, maybe not, Johnny. Maybe I was a little bit wrong and a little bit right."

"And there is nothing to be ashamed of in that. Most things in life have parts that are true and parts that are not true, depending on how you look at it. Being able to accept that fact can make life so much easier."

"But how does all that relate to why Stan didn't invite me to his party?" Righteous went on.

"The way we respond to people affects the way they feel about us. When we respond in positive ways, we invite people in and make them feel safe and respected by us. But when we respond in negative ways, we push people away. When you believe that your way is the only way, it is sure to affect how you relate and respond to others. That attitude is likely to make you not truly listen to other people's points of view because you are already convinced that your way is the right way. It is also likely to result in your being critical of other people when they disagree with you.

"One of the other things that happen when you see things in these kind of black-and-white ways is that you can get so stuck on the rules that you become rigid and no fun. While you need to have rules sometimes, having too many rules can make things really boring. Too many rules can kill all the creativity and playfulness in things. And talking too much about rules with friends can result in your friends starting to see you in the way they would see a parent rather than in the way they would see a peer."

"What do you mean? You think kids see me like a parent?"

"You always hear kids complain about how their parents are constantly telling them what they can and can't do, and about how they have to follow the rules.

"If a kid is always talking about rules, the other kids are probably going to start to see him as acting like their parents. And while parents can be great, you don't really want friends who are like your parents."

"What makes you think I'm doing that?" Righteous asked.

"You know, I talked to some of the guys from your old *World of Warcraft* clan. And you were right about your hunch. They didn't want you on the team any more. But they didn't want to hurt your feelings by telling you directly."

Righteous huffed and started cracking his knuckles again. This time it was definitely the 'I'm pissed off and I want to punch something' kind of knuckle cracking.

"That's messed up," he said in an angry voice. "I mean, I kind of figured that was the case, but to actually hear it's true makes me mad. They should have told me instead of playing games with me."

"I think you're right about that, Righteous. They probably should have told you directly. It's gotta hurt to hear that."

"So why then? Why didn't they want me on the team? Do they just hate me?" Righteous asked, clearly hurt.

"I think that if they really hated you, they wouldn't have cared about your feelings and probably would have told you straight out that they didn't want you on the team any more. That doesn't make it right that they lied to you. But I think it's important to know that it wasn't to hurt you.

"It seems clear that the main reasons they didn't want you on the team any more were all the things we've been talking about. They feel that you were rigid about rules and didn't listen to anyone else's opinion. They said that you frequently said that you were right and they were wrong. They also told me that your attitude took all the fun out of the game."

Righteous just sat there cracking his knuckles and staring at me. His face was wrinkled by emotion. Anger swirled around him in the silence. But, while there was silence on the outside, it was clear that there was a lot going on in the inside. I imagined a tornado of emotion twisting within.

"It's hard to hear all that, huh?" I asked.

"It makes me mad," Righteous said.

"And I imagine it hurts too, Righteous."

When I suggested to Righteous that he might also be feeling hurt, something shifted in him. He began to appear less angry and more sad.

"So is that why I wasn't invited to Stan's party?" he continued.

"That is definitely part of it. But I think that the biggest reason has to do with your style of being critical of things that you don't agree with. Things like, you know, the new Cheese Monkeys album."

I tilted my head back slightly and raised my eyebrows expectantly to feel out if he had heard the rumors about the party.

Righteous' eyes got big. "It's not really true, is it? They're not really going to play at his party are they, Johnny?"

It was hard to contain my excitement, and a big smile broke out on my face.

"No way!" Righteous said.

His reaction set off my own excitement about seeing the Cheese Monkeys, and I started to giggle. But I quickly caught myself, because this was in no way the right situation in which to be laughing.

For Righteous, this was a serious and painful matter, and for me to laugh would give the message that I was missing the whole feeling tone of the situation.

I straightened my body and cleared my throat, and spoke in a serious tone. "Let's just say they were playing. If they were, how do you think they might feel hearing your harsh critique of their new album? Can you imagine how Stan would feel if that happened at a party where the Cheese Monkeys did him the huge favor of playing?"

"I would never say that to them directly," Righteous said, with anguish in his voice. "That would be totally inappropriate, Johnny. I can't believe that Stan would think I would do something like that."

"But you did repeatedly say really nasty things about the album to everyone else," I reminded him. "Even when people started to get upset, you continued to tear the Cheese Monkeys apart. That might make people think you would do the same thing if you met the band."

"But I would … I would never … I mean, I still love the Cheese Monkeys. It's just that I was disappointed with how different their new album was. I would never …"

Righteous didn't know what to say. He was clearly upset, not only at the thought of being rejected by his friends, but also at the realization that his negative way of responding to people had resulted in his missing out on an incredible opportunity.

He slumped over and rubbed the palms of his hands against his forehead. "So I'm just a hopeless loser," he said in a pain-ridden voice.

"If you were hopeless, Righteous, I wouldn't be here talking to you. I wouldn't waste my time. Realizing the things you do to push people away isn't hopeless. It is the most hopeful thing you could do because, once you can identify a problem, there is the possibility that you can do something to make things better."

"I don't think there is anything I could do to make things better. There is no way Stan is going to invite me to his party given the way he sees me."

"That may be true, Righteous. But I don't think the party is what it's all about. The real issue has to do with your social life as a whole. Stan's party is just one piece in a much bigger picture. And I think that there are a lot of things you can do to make your social future more hopeful."

Righteous stopped rubbing his head and lifted his gaze up. He looked at me expectantly.

"Okay," he said. "I'm listening. If you have some social detective wisdom you think might help, let me have it."

"Well, let's start with the black-and-white thinking, because that seems to get you into a lot of trouble. The first step in dealing with black-and-white thinking is to notice when you're doing it. I'd recommend that whenever you are having strong opinions about something, you ask yourself some key questions to help you notice if you are thinking in an all-or-nothing, black-and-white way.

"You can ask yourself, 'Am I looking at things as either all right or all wrong?' You can ask yourself, 'Am I open to different possibilities or points of view, other than my own?' It would also be helpful to ask yourself, 'How might someone else see things differently than me?'

"In addition to asking yourself questions, I think it would be helpful to remind yourself about the stealing medicine situation from your debate. That is a great example of how the distinction between right and wrong is not really that clear, when you look at all the different points of view. Sometimes we can forget that there are different points of view, and reminding ourselves about a situation like your debate dilemma can help us to remember that there might be other points of view that are valid and important to consider.

"I would also encourage you to ask other people how they see things and listen carefully to what they have to say. Sometimes when you listen carefully and imagine exactly how someone else is seeing something, it can open up a whole new point of view that you might never have imagined."

"That makes sense, Johnny," Righteous admitted, "but it's hard because often when I start noticing other people's points of view I get anxious, so it is easier to just not think about how they see things.

"That's an awesome observation, Righteous, and it totally makes sense. I call that the 'bury your head in the sand' approach to anxiety. It's like what ostriches do when they sense danger. They bury their heads in the ground and just pretend the danger is not there.

"Often when people are anxious and don't have any good tools to deal with their anxiety, they do the same thing. They try their best to pretend that the thing that makes them anxious doesn't exist. But that strategy doesn't work that well. In fact, when it comes to anxiety, avoidance makes it worse. When you avoid something that makes you anxious, it actually makes you more anxious, which can lead to you avoiding it even more, which, of course, leads to being even more anxious.

"Often the only real way to overcome anxiety is to face the thing that makes you anxious. But you want to face the thing that makes you anxious armed with some good tools to deal with the anxiety.

"One thing that can help when you are anxious is noticing what your body is doing. Usually when we are anxious, our bodies get tense and uncomfortable. If you can notice where your body feels uncomfortable, you can do things to help your body feel better.

"For example, taking deep breaths is a great thing to do when your body is feeling tense and uncomfortable. You can also put your hand on the place where you are feeling tense, which can be soothing. I imagine that is part of what you were doing when you were rubbing your forehead before."

"Yeah, maybe," Righteous said. "But I wasn't really thinking about it."

"We do a lot of things without thinking about it. But when we are aware and thinking about those kinds of things, they work much better. After you do something to calm your body down, you can then do something to deal with the thoughts in your head that might be making you anxious. Frequently, we feel anxious because of the thoughts we are having.

"But just as some thoughts can make us more anxious, other thoughts can make us less anxious. I suggest that you have some thoughts in your toolbox that will make you less anxious when things are not as simple as you would like them to be."

Righteous asked, "What kind of thoughts would help?"

His question told me that he was paying attention to what I was saying, so I offered him some suggestions.

"There are a lot of different things you can think to yourself to help you feel less anxious when things are not black and white. You can tell yourself something like, 'It's okay if things seem a little complicated,' or 'I can handle not knowing the answer right now,' or 'Shades of gray don't have to be scary, they can be fun too.'

"You can remind yourself that the unknown can offer an interesting mystery to explore, and that the anxious feeling will go away if you just stick with it. You might also want to reassure yourself that you can handle different ways of looking at things, and that nothing bad is going to happen if the answer isn't clear right away.

"The point is that you want to be clear inside that you can tolerate the unknown. Reassuring yourself in ways like this can help you approach new information and different points of view in a way that is less stressful and more enjoyable.

"I think that if you are less anxious, you will also be less likely to talk in ways that are offensive to other people. When you're anxious, it often comes across as angry and harsh. Had I not known better, I would have thought you were really upset with me."

Wrinkling his brow in a way that communicated the frustration he seemed to be feeling, Righteous said, "Sometimes when I'm upset, I'm not even sure if it is anger or anxiety or something else I'm feeling. It just all gets mixed together."

"Well," I reassured him, "hopefully by dealing with your anxiety better, that won't happen as much. But there are other things you can do that would help you to communicate with people in a way that doesn't irritate them so much."

The Case of the Boy Who Couldn't Handle the Gray in Life

Righteous pulled out a pad of paper and a pen from his notebook. "You're giving me a lot of information," he said. "I'm going to have to take some notes, or I'll never remember it all."

"That is a great idea, Righteous," I countered and continued.

"So one of the things that I gather from talking with the guys from your *World of Warcraft* team is that people often don't feel you are really listening to their points of view. We just talked about how it's very important to listen to other people's points of view. But it's not enough just to listen. You have to let people know that you're listening.

"An effective and easy way to show people you've been paying attention to them is to give them a summary of what they said. You can say something like, 'So you are saying …,' or 'So your point is …'" This can help show the other person that you understand where they are coming from. And once you show someone that you understand their point of view, they will be more likely to listen to how you see things.

"I'd also recommend that you be very clear about what are facts and what are opinions, and that you stop referring to your opinions as facts."

Righteous looked up from the pad he was writing on with a questioning look on his face. That was my cue that I needed to explain what I meant, so I continued.

"I noticed you often state your opinion as if it were fact. Facts are things that can be measured and, for the most part, agreed upon by everyone. It is a fact that the sun is in the sky. We would all be able to observe that with our eyes and agree on it. It is a fact that the Cheese Monkeys just came out with a new album. There is undisputed evidence for that.

"But whether or not the sun looks beautiful in the sky, or whether or not the new Cheese Monkeys album is good are things that can be discussed. Those things are not facts. They are opinions. Facts are measurable things in the world. Opinions are based on how we as individuals think and feel about things.

"To say that the new Cheese Monkeys album is bad is your opinion. That conclusion is based on what you think and how you feel. It is not based on undisputable facts. But you frequently state opinions as facts, and when you do that, it's kind of like saying to other people that their opinions are not valid."

"But the new Cheese Monkeys album *is* bad," Righteous interrupted.

"No," I corrected him. "Your opinion is that it is bad. But in other people's opinions, it's really good. It's kind of like telling someone who loves strawberry ice cream that they are wrong for thinking strawberry ice cream is good, because you don't like it. It might be your opinion that strawberry is a bad flavor, but that does not make it a fact."

The Case of the Boy Who Couldn't Handle the Gray in Life

Righteous leaned his head to the side and nodded a little in agreement with what I was saying. It was an uncertain and slightly hesitating nod, but it was a shake nonetheless.

"Okay. I guess I get what you're saying. So should I just keep my mouth shut?" he asked.

"I'm not saying that. What I'm saying is that when you are expressing your opinion, you need to be clear that you realize it's your opinion and not a fact. So, for example, instead of saying, 'The fact is the new Cheese Monkeys album is terrible,' you could say, 'In my opinion, the new album is not as good as their old stuff.'

"Notice that I am not only making it clear that it is my opinion, I'm also not being as harsh and critical in the way I am expressing my feelings. Not being so harsh is also a really important thing to practice because, when our opinions are stated in a way that's too harsh, it can be extremely offensive to people.

"Finally, while I don't think there is necessarily a need to 'keep your mouth shut,' as you put it, I do think that once you have stated your opinion, you might want to let it go and move onto something else.

"One of the things I noticed in your interactions with people, and that the guys in your *World of Warcraft* group seemed to notice as well, is that you have a hard time letting go of things when people don't agree with you."

273

To expand on this topic, I went on. "I think it would be very helpful for you to practice saying something like, 'I guess we just see it differently,' and letting that type of comment be the end of the discussion, rather than continuing to argue your point of view."

Righteous continued to scribble in his notebook after I finished talking. I waited patiently as he wrote, going over his case in my head to see if there was anything else I needed to share with him. Finally, his pen came to a stop and his eyes rose to meet mine.

"Anything else?" he asked.

"One last point," I said.

Righteous looked at me, waiting to hear what I had to say.

This time it was my turn to pause as I thought of the best way to say what I was about to say. I went through a number of different ways I could make my final point, but I kept coming back to the following statement, which I said to Righteous with a friendly smile on my face and in a kind tone of voice.

"I think you need to loosen up a little, buddy."

Righteous seemed caught a little off guard by that one. His eyes got big. "Pardon me?" he said.

The Case of the Boy Who Couldn't Handle the Gray in Life

"Exactly!" I exclaimed.

"Kids don't really say things like 'pardon me,' Righteous. That's kind of what your grandpa says. I mean, I don't want to cramp your style or change who you are, but I think that if you tried to loosen up a little and not always be so formal, you would be more approachable to the other kids.

"I'm not telling you not to be yourself. But maybe you could try to reach outside the rules of properness a little, and throw in a 'what's up, dude' instead of a 'nice to see you,' or a high five instead of a formal handshake. Things like that. I think that would probably go a long way with the other kids."

Righteous' face relaxed; he seemed to be taking in what I was saying. He made another note on his pad, and then looked at me, which was my cue to continue.

"I think that covers it," I said. "We hit most of the main points."

Righteous closed his notebook, and we both stood up and brushed little crumbs of leaves off our pants.

 "Thank you for your help, Johnny," Righteous said, as he reached out his hand to shake mine.

I extended my hand to meet his but, as our palms moved closer to one another's, Righteous seemed to change his mind and lifted his hand up with his palm facing me, giving me the universal sign for a high five.

I smiled and slapped his hand with mine.

"Later, dude," he said.

"Smell you later, Righteous," I shot back, along with a smile and a laugh.

Another day in the life of a social detective, and another case cracked wide open.

Chapter 10

Chant of the Cheese Monkeys: The Case of Stan's Most Legendary Party Yet

had the incredibly good fortune of getting to see the Cheese Monkeys live last time they were in town. They played to a sold-out audience and, as bands often do, they went on late.

As the time went on and the audience kept waiting, they began chanting the words "Cheese Monkeys" over and over. At first it was a low murmur of a chant that faded in and out and overlapped with the random hoots and hollers from the crowd.

But as the wait continued, more and more people joined in until the chant was so loud and forceful that I could feel the rhythmic words in every inch of my body ... "Cheese Monkeys, Cheese Monkeys, Cheese Monkeys."

With each repetition of the chant, I became more and more excited until the lights finally went out and the crowd went crazy as the band strutted onto the stage and began to rock the night away.

Well, as it happened, I awoke today with that very same chant in my head: "Cheese Monkeys, Cheese Monkeys, Cheese Monkeys." Over and over again throughout the day: "Cheese Monkeys, Cheese Monkeys, Cheese Monkeys."

As I ate my Cheerios for breakfast, I could hear the words between crunches. As I rode my bike around the neighborhood, the words fell in synch with my pedaling. I could hear them in the shower and in between the heavy ticks and tocks of the grandfather clock in my dad's office. I could even hear the words over the sound of the lawnmower as I did my Saturday chores. "Cheese Monkeys, Cheese Monkeys, Cheese Monkeys."

You see, the school year was finally over, and today was the day that Stan was having his big party. And, of course, that meant it was the day the Cheese Monkeys were going to be playing live in Stan's backyard!

I usually try to come to parties just a little bit late. What they call "fashionably late." That way the social layout is already in place to some extent and you can sort of slip into the social stream that is already flowing. But today it was incredibly hard to do the fashionably late thing. In fact, it took all my willpower not to be the first one at Stan's door at seven PM.

I managed to hold out until almost quarter after seven. As I walked up the driveway, Stan was by the front door greeting guests. "Yo, Johnny!" he said in a loud, exuberant voice as he saw me approaching. "You made it."

The Case of Stan's Most Legendary Party Yet

"I wouldn't miss it for the world," I shot back as we high-fived each other.

"Come on in, Johnny. The party is just starting. My dad popped for pizzas and snacks. Come around the back and help yourself."

I walked down along the side of the house to the backyard. There was already a swarm of kids buzzing around. It's funny 'cauz for me this was in many ways the real graduation ceremony. We had the formal school graduation last week. Parents, teachers, formal attire, long inspirational speeches by kids. It was the celebration of another successful year of academic achievement and growth. It was great, and we were all proud to be advancing.

But Stan's year-end party was, in many ways, the celebration of our social accomplishments this year. From the point of view of a social detective, school is not just about learning facts and ideas. It's not just about learning how to be intellectually smart. It is also about learning how to be socially smart.

As I looked around the party, I saw so many familiar faces. Faces of people I'd known for years. Faces of people I'd had the good fortune of getting to know better this past year. And people I'd had the honor of working with to solve their social mysteries.

As I scanned the party, I saw Antonio laughing and joking around with Bobby and a group of other guys. I saw Summer huddled in a circle arm-and-arm with Anya, Kaia and Emma, whispering and giggling like they were the best friends in the world.

And Sora was there, surrounded by a group of kids reminiscing about the final playoff game. Sora had ended up getting to play in the last three games, and her skill and fresh, new sportsmanship gave the team the edge they needed to win the playoffs and move ahead to the state championships.

Mona and Sassy were also both there hanging out with friends. And Dimsly was … well, Dimsly was still Dimsly. He still seemed to have that sort of lost look most of the time. But he was understanding irony much, much better and, when he didn't quite get things, he was able to play it off much better, so others didn't really notice.

Even Billy had managed to turn things around and find better ways of getting attention. The undeniable evidence of that was that after many sincere apologies to kids like Stan, and months of proving himself, Stan had invited him to his party.

In some ways, I think Stan and Billy helped each other. Billy helped Stan to assert himself more, and Stan's deciding not to let Billy push him around any more helped Billy realize that he needed to treat people better if he ever wanted to have any real friends.

As I looked around at all the faces, I heard something beautiful. Even though the Cheese Monkeys would soon be stepping up to the makeshift stage Stan and his brother had set up, it was not the "Cheese Monkeys, Cheese Monkeys, Cheese Monkeys" chant that I was hearing. It was the beautiful sound of the social symphony. The harmonies, melodies and rhythms that can only be heard, felt and appreciated when people are interacting with one another. It was the most beautiful sound I had ever heard.

As I listened intently to those melodies, harmonies and rhythms, I saw Righteous coming up Stan's driveway. He spotted me right away, smiled and came over.

"Hey, Johnny."

"Hey, Righteous. Glad you could make it."

"Me too, Johnny. After you and I talked, I did a lot of thinking. And I have really been trying to make some changes."

"That's great, Righteous," I said with a smile.

"Yeah and hey, huh, what time is it, Johnny?"

I looked at my watch. "It's ... hey, it's 7:25. Mr. Preachly, I do believe you are late!" I said.

"Yup. Is that fashionably late enough for you, Johnny?"

We laughed. "I'd say so. I take it you patched things up with Stan," I said.

"Yeah. Stan is a pretty cool guy. He was really understanding. He even talked to the other guys who I used to play *World of Warcraft* with. We all got together, and I let them know I was sorry and could understand why they did not want me to play with them any more. And you know what they did?"

"No. What?" I asked.

"They asked if I wanted to give it another try. Can you believe that? After all that, they invited me back to play with them!"

"That doesn't surprise me at all, Righteous. Taking responsibility for your actions and letting people know what you did wrong is a powerful thing. People respect that, and it helps them to trust you. That is so cool, Righteous. I'm really happy for you."

"Thanks, Johnny. Really. Thank you so much. I could never have done it without you."

Righteous' eyes seemed to soften their focus some, the way eyes often do when someone is thinking. It was as if Righteous' eyes were looking inside to his thoughts, even though they were still resting their gaze on me.

After a long pause, he spoke. "I have a question for you, Johnny. How did you figure all this stuff out? I mean, I would never in a million years have seen all the things you saw happening with me. I would never in a million years have been able to figure out the social world the way you have."

His question caught me a little off guard. It was a great question. But it was one with a very lengthy answer. It was an answer that would tell the tale of a boy who struggled for a long time to understand his own social world. A tale that, if fully told, would speak of countless hours of mapping out and investigating his own personal social mysteries.

For too many years, my story was one of someone who felt completely alone and hopeless about ever having friends and being happy. But fortunately my tale had a happy ending. As I became more aware of myself and of the world around me, my hopelessness transformed into hope. And my greatest weakness became my greatest teacher, enabling me to discover my own strengths.

Without my social weakness, I would probably never have fully discovered the potential I had inside of me. And I most definitely would never have become a social detective.

I could sense the focus of my eyes softening as I turned my attention to my own thoughts and feelings, trying to think of how best to answer a question that for me was not as simple as it might seem.

But eventually I brought my attention back to Righteous, and my eyes once again focused on him.

"I figured it out by staying alert and not giving up when things seemed too complicated and mysterious. I figured it out because, even when the shades of gray made things seem complex and overwhelming, I still had hope that an answer would come if I just kept trying to be aware of myself and the world around me.

"And I would bet that you could figure these kinds of things out yourself, Righteous, in much less than a million years. Most people are more capable of solving their social mysteries than they realize. Sometimes they just need a little help figuring out how to be their own social detective."

"And that's where you come in, huh, Johnny?"

"Yup. That's where I come in."

Righteous smiled and high-fived me. "Well then, I guess I'll be smelling you later, Johnny," he said.

"Not if I smell you first," I shot back, and we both laughed.

I spotted a group of friends I'd not talked to in a while and decided to join in their social symphony. As I walked toward them, I thought about all the kids who had come to me for help in the past year. The school year was over, and it had been a good year in so many ways.

But the best thing for me this year was being able to help so many kids find their way out of the darkness of their social mysteries. For someone like me, who knows first-hand how hard it can be to struggle socially, it's the best experience you could imagine.

… Even better than seeing the Cheese Monkeys live and up close in Stan's backyard.

Solving Your Own Social Mysteries in 10 Easy Steps

Good social detectives never stop learning. They keep their minds open and always try to think about the feedback they get from others. During my interactions with Righteous, he asked me to give him feedback on his case in writing.

As I thought about what Righteous had said, I realized that this was an excellent idea. I often give people a lot of information, and sometimes it can be overwhelming. So I've decided that it would be helpful to give people something in writing that they can refer back to.

Below is a form that I've made that I now give to all of my clients. The form helps my clients see how I go about solving social mysteries so that they can get a better sense of how they can start to solve their own mysteries. I've used Antonio's case as an example.

I've also added a blank form in case you would like to try your hand at some detective work. In addition to being helpful for clients, the form is an excellent tool to help you practice your own social detective skills and solve your own mysteries.

The truth is everyone has a social detective within them. Sometimes it just takes practice to let it out. And I could use the help because there are a lot of mysteries out there to be solved. So if you're interested in building your own detective skills, try to solve some mysteries of your own. And please feel free to come and visit me any time. I'd love to hear about the mysteries you're working on. You can find me at www.socialdetectives.com.

Sample Worksheet for Solving Social Mysteries

Too Close for Comfort: The Case of Back-Away Bobby

1. *Identify the problem:*
    Antonio's problem is that his friend keeps backing away from him and not wanting to play with him.

2. *Identify the social mystery:*
    Since Antonio and Bobby seem to be friends, it is a mystery why Bobby is backing away and not wanting to play.

3. *List the facts:*
    - Bobby often pulls away from Antonio.

    - Bobby seems friendly when he first sees Antonio.

    - Antonio greets Bobby by putting his hands on his shoulders.

    - Antonio wraps his legs around Bobby.

    - Bobby pulls away.

    - Antonio gets more and more excited.

    - Bobby gets less and less excited.

    - Bobby's mood seems to change, and he does not smile as much.

- Bobby moves away.

- Antonio moves closer.

- The two seem to play nicely together.

After just a short time of playing, Bobby waves to Antonio and runs off to the other end of the playground. Antonio looks sad.

4. *Organize the facts:*
   Bobby seems happy to see Antonio at first but then gets less and less happy, and after only a short time he runs off.

   As Antonio gets more and more excited, he seems to make more physical contact with Bobby. When this happens, Bobby seems to pull away and become less happy.

5. *Imagine and describe how others might see the problem:*
   How might Bobby feel: Bobby's pulling away from Antonio might mean that he does not like to be so physically close. Maybe he feels crowded. It also seems that he might not like it when Antonio is so excitable. Maybe he feels over-whelmed when Antonio is so energetic.

6. *List things that might have caused the problem:*
   It seems like Antonio's problem of Bobby pulling away from him is really being caused by the problem Antonio has with personal space. So it would make sense that if he can solve the problem with personal space, the other prob-lem might go away.

7. *List possible solutions or remedies to the problem:*
   a. Antonio could stop playing with Bobby. Then he would not have to worry about getting in Bobby's space or about feeling rejected by Bobby.

   b. Antonio could tell Bobby he needs to relax and not worry so much about people getting in his space.

   c. Antonio could find ways to give other people more personal space. He could do this by noticing how close he is to others. For example he could use the one arm's length technique. He could also make a point to notice other people's reactions to him.

8. *List the possible pros and cons for each solution/remedy:*
   Solution 1
   - The pros of stopping playing with Bobby is that he could make sure he did not get in his personal space any more, and Bobby would probably not get irritated by that any more. Also, this solution might keep Antonio from having to feel rejected by his friend every day.

   - But the cons would be that Antonio would not really be facing the problem and he would lose his friendship with Bobby.

   - Also, it is likely that even though Antonio would not be playing with his friend and being rejected every day, he still might feel rejected. In fact, he might feel even more rejected at not seeing his friend at all. He would also not have the opportunity to deal with his problem with personal space, and it would most likely come out in future friendships. *The cons outweigh the pros.*

Solution 2

- The pros of telling Bobby to relax are that Antonio would not have to put any effort into dealing with his problem with personal space. It is possible this approach might help Bobby to relax and accept Antonio more.

- The cons are that Antonio would not have the opportunity to deal with his problem with personal space, and he would be practicing a bad habit of blaming others for his problems. Also, it is likely that Bobby would get irritated with Antonio's blaming him for a problem that was clearly Antonio's. People usually do not tend to respect people who blame others for their problems so it is likely that Bobby would lose respect for Antonio. *The cons outweigh the pros.*

Solution 3

- The pros of Antonio taking responsibility for his problem with personal space and taking steps to deal with the problem are that he would be addressing the problem head on. He would learn strategies for dealing with his problem. Because he would be taking responsibility for his problem, he would not lose respect and would probably actually gain respect from Bobby. It would probably significantly increase the quality of his friendship with Bobby. The cons are that it would take effort. *The pros outweigh the cons.*

9. *After testing out the top remedies, write down if they were successful and if there were any positive or negative effects of the solution/remedies:*

In the end, Antonio used the remedies Johnny suggested. He found that they were very helpful. Sometimes he would forget to use them, but he would eventually notice the feedback from others, which helped him to remember to keep an eye on his personal space. The remedies had very positive effects on his friendship with Bobby. Bobby stopped backing away, and the two spent much more time together. Antonio noticed it also helped in other friend-ships. Antonio did not notice any negative effects of the remedies.

10. *Use the information from these tests to develop even better remedies:*
In Antonio's case, the remedies seemed to be effective. The one problem he had was that he sometimes forgot about personal space and only remembered when he start-ed getting negative feedback from people. Perhaps Anto-nio could try to remind himself more about the importance of personal space so that he did not forget when he was playing with friends.

Worksheet for Solving Social Mysteries

1. *Identify the problem:*

2. *Identify the social mystery:*

3. *List the facts:*

4. *Organize the facts:*

5. *Imagine and describe how others might see the problem:*

6. *List things that might have caused the problem:*

7. *List possible solutions or remedies to the problem:*

8. *List the possible pros and cons for each solution/remedy:*

9. *After testing out the top remedies, write down if they were successful and if there were any positive or negative effects of the solution/remedies:*

10. *Use the information from these tests to develop even better remedies:*

If you would like to learn more about what Johnny is up to, and about how you too can become a social detective, come visit Johnny online at www.socialdetectives.com

P.O. Box 23173
Overland Park, Kansas 66283-0173
www.aapcpublishing.net